ANDREW D. WASHTON

What Happens Next?

STORIES TO FINISH FOR INTERMEDIATE WRITERS

TEACHERS COLLEGE PRESS

Teachers College, Columbia University

New York/London

ISBN 0-8077-2454-8

Published by Teachers College Press,
1234 Amsterdam Ave., New York, New York 10027.

Manufactured in the United States of America
Designed by David Miller

*To my wife, Ruth, who worked so closely
with me on the manuscript for this book*

*And to Professor Irwin Stark of the
City College of New York*

Contents

To the Teacher

One of the first things I learned, as a teacher in an urban school (and this no doubt applies in any school), was that there are certain words that, when used by a teacher, are virtually guaranteed to produce instant adverse pupil reaction. One, "homework," is, of course, anathema; another is "composition." All pupils know that during the first week of school they will be asked to write a composition titled something like "How I Spent My Summer Vacation." After Christmas or Easter holiday, they will write "How I Spent My Holiday Vacation." The fact that the composition assignment, whatever boring topic it is, is invariably followed by the question, "How much do we got to write?" indicates that, on an interest scale, composition-writing is rated by pupils somewhere between alphabetizing words and practicing cursive x's.

I came to realize, very early in my teaching career, that something had to be done to change the prevailing attitudes towards composition writing (of both teachers and pupils). Merely replacing the word "composition" by "story" wasn't nearly enough. I had to find some method to spark the children's interest. To use the professional educators' favorite word, I had to find a way to *motivate* the children. (I myself, by the way, prefer the word stimulate.)

The method I eventually found to be most successful is really quite a simple one. Essentially: I read to the class a good story that leads up to a crucial point—and breaks off. What happens next? The children decide, and provide endings to the stories.

I wrote the half-stories myself. Since I knew my pupils, what was on their minds, and what got them excited—*stimulated*—I was able to provide story-situations that the children could relate to, with protagonists that they could understand and identify with. (Of course, not too many years ago, I was an elementary school student myself, and I haven't forgotten what was on my mind, or on my friends' minds, in those days.) I was happily amazed to receive, in some cases, pages of work from pupils who had rarely put a pencil to a piece of paper. I personally feel that composition writing has sunk so low in pupil estimation because it has become so formal. Many teachers, including several who taught me, and several I later taught with, are so caught up in the mechanics of the subject, *i.e.* margins, skipped lines, neatness, etc., and spend so much time on it, that they forget the primary purpose of the lesson: to get pupils to express ideas, thoughts, emotions, feelings, in writing. What the child's paper looks like is less important than what he or she says. Of course, form is important, too.

The teachers who read the stories that follow, many of which were tried and used successfully in various classrooms, will not find too many typical or overused story ideas. Some, of course, will be traditional, and familiar, and there are some that are related to social studies or science curricula, and can be used in conjunction with certain lessons in these areas. But many of the central ideas and problems presented in these tales are drawn from the ideas and problems of my own pupils, or from my own memories.

Procedure

I structure my lessons this way:

• On the chalkboard, I write *What Happens Next?* I never, never use the word "Composition." It's good, I have found, for the pupils to be slightly perplexed by the three words on the chalkboard, and for them to wonder, "What the heck do those words mean?" Keep them in suspense for a few moments.

• I explain to the class that I will read them a story, but that it is not a complete story. It doesn't have an ending. They will write the ending for the story. The first time this lesson is used there will always be a few pupils who really don't understand what is wanted. For them, I use this example: "Suppose you are watching a cops and robbers show on television. (The name of any currently popular show can be used.) You know that the action will go on and on and then suddenly, just at the exciting point—the commercial! And you wonder to yourself, now what's going to happen? Well, I'm going to read you a story, and just where the commercial will cut in, I'll stop, and you'll finish the story!"

• If the teacher wishes to introduce the concept of completing an incomplete story gradually to his or her class, there are various ways in which this may be done. For instance, the day before the half-story lesson exercise is to be used for the first time, the teacher may create a similar but briefer exercise using, for instance, some of the week's spelling words or material from the new social studies lesson.

> *Teacher:* I'll read half a paragraph to you. You try to finish it, using one or more of the week's spelling (or social studies) words.

> "The crew on Columbus' ship was very weary. They had been at sea for months! Food was running low and the men were angry. There was talk of mutiny. Finally, one morning, a sailor high up in the crow's nest spotted land. 'Land!' he cried. Then . . ."

This sort of exercise can be done more than once, to familiarize the class with the procedure of listening and then writing answers. The familiarization does not have to be done with spelling words or social studies lessons, of course. Science and current events lend themselves to this kind of exercise. The very brief stories given on pages 27 to 29 can also be used for this purchase. The next time this kind of lesson is used, it won't be necessary to spend much time on a review of procedures. I found that because the pupils enjoyed themselves so much the first time they were actually eager to hear another half-story.

• Next, I explain that the story I am going to read has no title. It's up to the students to make up an appropriate one. (In slower classes, however, I've found that it may be better to provide one. It gives the pupils a little "direction" for their writing.) I make it clear that there is no "official" ending to the story. This eliminates a fear many pupils harbor—that they won't write what the teacher wants. Make it clear to the pupils that you want originality and imagination. Tell them: "Surprise me!"

• I usually read each story twice, and ask the pupils not to begin writing (although many are eager to) until I've reread the story. This will enable the students to grasp details of plot, narrative, and characterization.

• It is extremely important to read the stories to the class with as much narrative exaggeration and flair as possible (within reasonable limits). Distinguish clearly between voices, good guys and bad guys, girls and boys. When appropriate, ham it up!

• You may find that some pupils will be so stimulated that they will not finish within the allotted time. This is a consummation devoutly to be wished!

• A follow-up lesson of reading the completed stories can be very enjoyable. All pupils love to read their (corrected and marked) responses to the class.

A Few Things to Keep in Mind

This sort of lesson works well because children love to listen to stories—and they love to use their imaginations. The teacher must know his or her pupils well before reading one of the stories to them. Nothing will fall flatter than a half-tale that a student finds boring, irrelevant, or beyond his or her ken, socially or intellectually. It follows that the teacher must be familiar with the story he or she uses. Brief summaries of all the half-stories in this book have been provided because, as the stories have no titles, the teacher will otherwise find it necessary to read each story in its entirety before deciding whether or not to use it. Some teachers may not want to use a story about stealing, for instance, and thus, from the summary, will eliminate it at once.

Pass out paper first, before explaining what the lesson is all about. It's better for the children to have paper on their desks when the story breaks off. Then, they can go right to work!

To facilitate writing for slower classes, the teacher might prepare in advance a chart or write on the chalkboard some of the more difficult names and places and other words the pupils are likely to ask how to spell. This will eliminate an awful lot of frustration. There is no reason why a teacher, reading one of the half-tales in the book, cannot modify certain phrases, words, and even sentence structure, to better meet the needs of the pupils.

What Can the Teacher Expect?

There are many factors at work. Teaching is like a bank account. You take out what you put in, plus interest. Children are extremely sensitive and will consciously or unconsciously pick up their teacher's attitudes, confidence (or lack of it), fears, prejudice, interest, or lack of it. Enthusiasm is a very contagious quality and the teacher who really possesses such a quality will usually have many fewer paper airplanes to duck during the course of a school day (to look at it one way). In other words, lessons will succeed if the teacher likes and enjoys the lessons, too. Substitute teachers (and these half-story lessons are very helpful for substitutes) know well how pupils respond to lessons or "work" meant to keep them occupied or busy: they hate it. It is hard to look pupils in the eye when explaining to them why they must do some sort of useless busywork.

The half-story lessons are fun. Teachers like them and pupils like them. The results will demonstrate this. In a sense, pupils are being "tricked" into writing stories, and using their imagination, but the end justifies the means.

The results will be a function of the teacher's sincerity, interest, and enthusiasm: $R = f(TS + TI + TE)$. The results will also be a function of what the stories mean to the children, how they relate to the social and economic context of each story. We must be honest and admit that some pupils are brighter than other pupils (or, to put it another way, some pupils are not as bright as others) and that while a certain group of pupils may pick up on subtlety, metaphor, and sarcasm, other pupils won't. It is painful to accept that pupils of or below a certain intellectual level cannot understand subtlety, sarcasm, metaphor. They take everything they hear (or read) literally. A teacher must really know her/his pupils well before choosing a tale to read. Certain groups of children will not only become bored, they will become *angry* when they do not understand what is being read to them. This response may come from the idea that is drummed into every pupil's head as soon as he or she enters school: "I must produce. I'm supposed to understand. If I don't, I'm stupid. I'm inferior." A size ten hat doesn't fit too well on a size seven skull, nor will a size five. The stories must fit well, like hats or shoes, not only intellectually but socio-economically. One of the professional educator's favorite words is *relevance*, and it certainly applies to the stories in this book. Chances are that a teacher in the Kansas Corn Belt won't get very good results by reading a class the half-story about a power failure in the New York City subway. (On the other hand, one might! Imagine what kids in Kansas could dream up about being stuck in a subway—considering the wonderful press "big cities" get all over the country!)

Evaluating Results: What to Mark For

Teachers must evaluate the results obtained from the half-story technique by comparing them to what their pupils normally produce.

A one-half page response from a child who barely or rarely writes more than his or her heading is a tremendous piece of work—regardless of whether he or she spells every other word incorrectly, or fails to keep margins, or skip lines. In other words (this may sound somewhat rhetorical) gauge the results not against some abstract model of perfection, but against work that has been done before.

Gifted children may produce novelettes; slower children may produce a few sentences, but keep in mind that something wonderful has been achieved when very slow or reluctant pupils suddenly realize that writing can be fun, and even a pleasure, and that their teacher is *pleased* by their efforts, so pleased that the pupils can (finally) feel justifiably proud of their accomplishments.

Grammar, sentence structure, and spelling are important, yet can a teacher affix a failing grade to a composition of one page, in which many words are incorrectly spelled, and punctuation is absent, handed in by a pupil who has never written more than five lines? "Effort" is as important as the final, formal result in such an instance. That pupil has taken a tremendous step forward.

Mark (if you must mark) each composition as an individual entity. Compare it with the work the student produced before. That is a sure way to gauge progress.

The Follow-Up Lesson

Reluctant writers seldom need encouragement to read their stories to the class. Sometimes the students' desire to read their responses is so great that, to avoid the moans and groans of disappointed would-be readers, the teacher must firmly announce that only a certain number of stories can be read.

As a general rule, it is best that the teacher read all the responses the day they are written, so the follow-up lesson can occur the next day.

Begin the follow-up lesson by reading a synopsis of the story to refresh the students' minds. Then call pupils up to read their endings. If a normally unproductive pupil has produced a good piece of work, be sure that he or she has a turn. The teacher's enthusiasm will be a great factor in encouraging a shy or reluctant pupil to read his or her work.

Other Suggestions

Some teachers may feel that certain of the stories lend themselves to dramatization. Plot endings may be worked out imaginatively in front of the class, rather than on paper.

Effective oral lessons may be developed from some of the stories in this book. Many of them deal with moral and ethical questions, which of course can be discussed.

The teacher may find that after this sort of half-story stimulus has been used successfully several times, pupils will want to write their own half-stories for the class to finish.

Arts and crafts activities can be developed in conjunction with many of the stories in the book; for instance, many children will like to draw or paint illustrations to accompany their story endings. Poor writers may express themselves best by illustrations and paintings.

Finally, if a teacher has the will and the means, some of the half-stories can be reproduced by stencil or rexograph with space at the end appropriate for the story ending. Slower students can then read along with the teacher, or take turns reading out loud. The pupils in brighter classes may work on their own, independently.

A Few Final Words

Many of these stories were written especially for the pupils in a so-called "inner-city" school, where the achievement level was low. The first story used in these classes was the one about a young child who moves to a new neighborhood and is afraid to go downstairs because he or she is afraid of the other kids on the block (page 92). The class, previously incredibly apathetic toward composition, really woke up. They produced wonderful work. They actually *asked me* for more lessons like the ones described above!

Gradually the half-stories moved out of the inner-city. The stories in this book are intended for pupils all over the country, city kids and country kids and suburban kids.

The stories are arranged approximately in the order of difficulty. More complex situations, characterizations, and plot subtlety will be found in the later stories. Plot summaries for all the stories in this book follow.

Plot Summaries

For simplicity's sake, the pronoun "he" is used in these summaries to describe a protagonist who may be of either sex. Otherwise, the protagonist's name will indicate his or her gender.

awkward position when his cousin saddles up a pony for him.   **30**

7   The family goes camping deep in the woods, so deep into the forest that all sorts of wild animals may be encountered, according to dad. The oldest child has a little trouble falling to sleep, and, just as he does, he hears some strange noises outside his tent.   **31**

8   While the children are feeding peanuts to the elephants at the zoo, Doris gets so close that an elephant snatches her straw hat right off her head.   **32**

9   Mrs. Marzipan, the most wonderful teacher in the school, hurts her ankle during Christmas holiday. Until she recovers, the class will have as a substitute a new teacher, a strange, nervous young man.   **34**

10   A young person and his friend occasionally play hooky from school when it gets too boring. Usually they concoct satisfactory explanations for their absences. This time, however, the teacher phones the mother at work *the same afternoon.*   **35**

11   A young person and his brother take a trip to the beach and the amusement park. The little boy is fascinated by the fire-eater so the older child leaves him alone for a minute to buy some ice cream. When the child returns, the little boy is gone!   **37**

12   A child, finally old enough to have a puppy of his own, takes loving care of it, but one day the dog is gone—the screen door wasn't snapped shut!   **39**

13   The new boy in class, Douglas, is ostracized because he's so "strange." But he gets a chance to prove himself when he comes to bat in the punch-ball game in a crucial situation.   **42**

14   The Indians on the island of "Manhatta," as they call it, live peacefully. One day a great ship carrying some strange people appears in the river, and announces its presence by blowing off the tops of some trees with a cannon shot.   **45**

15   A young child steals baseball cards from the dime store, so as to have just as many as the other kids. But one day his secret is discovered and two of his friends threaten to tell his mother. Terrified, he runs upstairs to safety. Then, a minute later, the doorbell rings.   **47**

16   The young deer's first year of life is relatively safe and peaceful. One afternoon, two young hunters suddenly acquaint it with some hard facts of life.   **49**

17   With his birthday only two weeks away, the young child wonders why no preparations are being made for a party. Mom and dad are strangely silent on the subject. With some help from the neighborhood genius, the child becomes convinced that he is going to have a *surprise* party! At last, the day arrives . . .   **52**

18   The woman the children call "the Nosey Lady" watches the street from her window all day long, and tells one child's mother if she sees the child do anything wrong; she's their next-door neighbor. But one afternoon she disappears from her window. This means freedom to transgress—or so it seems.   **55**

19   Ed falls in love with the new girl in the class, Cindy. She's quiet and shy and so is he. He sends her, anonymously, little gifts and poems. No one suspects him, of course, after the teacher intercepts one of his messages. One day, as he sits under a tree composing a poem, some other pupils dash out and snatch the paper from his hand!   **57**

20   Patricia is a very, very annoying girl. Finally she provokes the teacher into throwing her out of the room, because she had taken another pupil's personalized pencils. Patricia blames this child for getting her into trouble and vows to get revenge. **60**

21 The superintendent of the apartment building, Josie, is a strange and scary lady who lives in the basement with her big dog. One evening, a child taking down the trash accidentally locks himself in the cellar and makes enough noise to rouse Josie from her sleep. **64**

22 Mom's birthday is coming up, but the protagonist of the story has only one dollar and seventeen cents with which to buy her a gift. Rats! Then, good news! Mom announces that rich old Uncle Nathan is coming for dinner that night. And Uncle Nathan always has gifts for everybody! Sometimes he gives money to the children, but he's a funny old man, and who knows what he'll pull out of his pocket? **66**

23 The neighborhood is safe, but recently a few robberies have taken place. The protagonist decides to keep an old golf club of dad's near his bed, just in case. One night he hears a funny noise coming from downstairs! **69**

24 Mrs. Marzipan's class studies space travel, and many of the children become interested in space travel, and the question of whether flying saucers exist. Two good friends, Ruth and Andy, take opposite views on the subject. Andy pooh-poohs the whole idea. One Saturday morning, as he bikes to the lake to fish, he comes upon a very strange object in an empty field. **72**

25 The protagonist of this story knows he's no angel, and he knows that to go on the great trips his teacher has planned, he has to reform his behavior drastically. To his great surprise, he is permitted to go along on the wonderful trip to the Museum of Natural History. All goes well until, as the class rushes out of the museum to catch the bus back to school, he sneaks off the line and inadvertently locks himself in the bathroom. **75**

26 A group of boys and girls hangs around the park after school every afternoon, watching some older children play ball—and smoke. It's not long before *they* attempt to look and act older by smoking in the park. One night, one member of the group sits by his bedroom window, smoking, and accidentally starts a fire. 78

27 A very well-behaved and polite child rather reluctantly agrees to go along, as an observer, on a shoplifting expedition to the dime store. He wants to show the other boys and girls that he's not a "chicken." Much to his dismay, the thieving party is spotted, and he, the observer, is the only one nabbed by the store's security guard. 80

28 Dad collects valuable old comic books, and guards his collection zealously. He hardly lets his own children look at them! One morning, to impress his classmates, the narrator sneaks some comics out of the house and brings them in to school. Unfortunately the teacher, Mrs. Anderson, is not amused or interested in such things as *Uncle Scrooge Number One* and takes the comics away and locks them in her closet. She will not return them, she says, without a note from his father. 83

29 The quietest, neatest section in the room is absolutely ruined when Mrs. Marzipan puts Peter in it. He continually annoys everyone. Mrs. Marzipan seems not to notice, as she is preoccupied with the other more overt troublemakers. The narrator of the story puts up with Peter's annoyances until one day Peter gets him so angry he finally loses his temper, takes matters into his own hands—and gets in trouble. 87

30 A group of boys and girls on a picnic decide to explore the large, mysterious wooded island in the middle of a lake. They have heard so many tales about it! To their dismay, after they have rowed to the island and landed, their boat drifts off, stranding them. 89

31   A child moves to a new, strange neighborhood. He is afraid to go outside to play—a gang of children seems to rule the street, intimidating youngsters and adults alike. So he stays in the house, until one morning mother finally orders him out. Downstairs, no one is about. The street seems quiet and safe—for a few minutes. The child hears a shout and turns around to see a group of boys and girls emerge from a building across the street.   **92**

32   Ruth had always loved the play *Peter Pan*. She tries out for a role in the school production but to her disappointment, all she lands is an understudy's part. She's so disappointed that, although she learns this role, she doesn't even plan to attend the PTA show. That night she stays home and watches television. The phone rings. It is Mrs. Strang, the teacher in charge of the annual play, and she is very excited.   **95**

33   The subway is late, and the narrator must get home, to study for two tests he has the next day. He also has a nervous, overprotective mother. Finally, the train arrives, jammed, of course. He gets on. The train runs for a few minutes, then stops in a tunnel. Soon, its lights begin to fade out. Power failure!   **98**

34   After his mother dies, the child and his father experience all sorts of difficulties. They move to a smaller apartment. Dad's health begins to decline. In his new school, the child's behavior deteriorates, and letters home from his teacher don't help dad's health. His boss warns him that if he takes too many sick days, he'll have to fire him. One afternoon at 3:15, the child is about to remove from the mailbox a letter home from his teacher, to prevent his father from seeing it. He is very surprised to see his father enter the lobby of the apartment building. He is home hours earlier than usual. He hugs the child to him.   **101**

35   A child wishes to give his Aunt Sarah, with whom he lives, a wonderful Christmas present, but the gift he wants to buy for her costs three dollars more than he has saved up. One day, about a week before Christmas, as the child heads home after buying some groceries in friendly Mr. Walters's neighborhood grocery, he discovers that Mr. Walters has given him too much change.   *104*

36   Father sells his cleaning store and the family moves to a new neighborhood where he plans to open a card and gift shop. Sadly, the deal falls through and father can't seem to establish another business. He sits around the house, and becomes more and more withdrawn. Various family problems develop. One night the children hear shouts from their parents' bedroom. They are scared. Then, they hear a loud crash and a thump. Father comes out, dressed, and without saying a word, leaves the house.   *107*

37   James Baxter grew up in the whaling town of New Bedford, Massachusetts, and looks forward to the day when he'll be old enough to go to sea on a whaling ship. At last that day comes. His father signs him up for a voyage on the *Bully Boy*. James is eager to see some action, and bothers an old sailor with his questions. Finally one day whales are spotted and James is allowed to row in one of the long boats. But the sea is rough and his feet get tangled in the harpoon line as a great sperm whale rises out of the sea and the harpooner gets ready to strike.   *110*

38   Bunk R, for various reasons, does not want to go to the Saturday night dance, but their counselor, Terry, has them over a barrel. If they don't go they'll get peanut butter sandwiches instead of turkey for Sunday dinner. Terry makes sure, in advance, that each boy will have a partner at the dance. Tommy, the most stubborn member of the bunk, winds up with "Calamity Jane."   *113*

39   Tom and Ellen sell their business and go to California

· 23 ·

during the Gold Rush. After a lot of hard work, they strike gold—but who are the three strangers on horses heading for the little valley in which they've worked so hard?

40 While the starship *Venturer* rockets through the universe at half the speed of light, seeking a planet similar to earth, its one-man crew is frozen, in suspended animation. At last, a planet is found and the astronaut is awakened by the ship's computers. As he gets his body and mind back into shape, he wonders: what kind of life will I find when I land? Soon he boards a small shuttle rocket, separates from the *Venturer* and heads for a landing on the new mysterious world, so far from earth.

Stories to Finish

1

My uncle decided to teach me how to fish. "I want you to be as good a fisherman as I am!" he said.

We walked to the pond. My uncle showed me how to set up the fishing pole, how to bait the hook, and how to cast the line. Finally I was ready. My uncle said, "Okay, now this is your first try! You probably won't catch a thing today, but you're just a beginner. When you're experienced like me, you'll really catch fish! Ready? Cast!"

I cast—and as soon as the baited hook hit the water, I felt a terrific tug on the line!

2

My camp-mates and I were hiking through the woods. We were enjoying ourselves. The weather was perfect, and it was too early in the afternoon for the biting flies and the mosquitos to bother us. We carried long thin poles, which we used as walking sticks.

We had crossed a stream and were heading up a low hill when I spotted an animal in the bushes only a few feet ahead of us.

"Look there!" I called out. "There's a rabbit in the bushes!" I poked at it with my stick.

"What are you doing?" yelled the counselor. "That's no rabbit; it's a skunk!"

3

I was really hungry when I got home from school yesterday afternoon. I opened the front door, dropped my books on the table, and yelled, "Mom, I'm home! I'm hungry!"

There was no answer. My mother wasn't in the house. "She's probably out shopping or visiting a neighbor," I thought. "And I need a snack!"

I walked into the kitchen—and there on the table was a juicy red still-warm cherry pie!

I stared at the pie.

"I'm awful hungry," I said to myself. "I think I'll cut myself just one tiny piece . . ."

4

She was very tired, but my mother still had to go out to buy groceries. As she put on her coat, she said to me, "Please behave yourself while I'm out! I have to go shopping. When I get back, I have a whole basket of ironing to do!"

"Okay, Mom," I promised. "I'll be good!"

She went out. She looked so tired, I thought. What could I do to help out? "I know!" I said to myself. "I'll help her with the ironing!"

Well, I had never ironed anything before in my life,

but I had watched my mom many times, so I got out the board, set it up, and plugged in the iron. Then I poked through the laundry basket. What would I do first? I pulled out one of my dad's white shirts. "I'll do this first!" I thought.

I turned the iron to "cotton" and spread the shirt out flat on the board. When it got hot, I began to iron. It was pretty easy!

The doorbell rang.

"Rats!" I said. I put the iron down and went to answer the bell. It was two of my friends, Freddy and Sheila.

"Hi!" I said. "Come on in! I'm helping my mom iron!"

"Hi!" said Freddy. "What's that funny burning smell?"

5

One afternoon, just as Mrs. Marzipan began to pass out paper for our spelling pretest, there were three knocks on the classroom door, Knock! Knock! Knock! and in strode Mr. Gribbins, the principal!

The class hadn't been making much noise, but all of a sudden the room became silent as a tomb. We were all scared of Mr. Gribbins. He *loved* to write notes home to parents, asking them in to school. He was *mean*.

Mrs. Marzipan said, "Hello, Mr. Gribbins. Won't you sit down?" He nodded hello, walked to the back of the room, and sat down at the library table. He took a little green notebook and a shiny silver pen from the inside pocket of his sports jacket.

Mrs. Marzipan said, "Class, because we are so honored to have Mr. Gribbins visit us, we'll have our test later! Instead, let's all take out our notebooks and open to the science homework. Let's see, who will read their report first? How about you?"

She smiled and pointed at *me!* I gulped. Then I looked back at Mr. Gribbins. His little notebook was open. His eyes were icy blue, staring at me. I turned away and opened *my* notebook. The class was quiet, waiting.

I fumbled through the pages. Where was my homework? Oh, no! I remembered. I left it on the kitchen table!

6

I had only been on a horse once—when I was very young I had had my picture taken while sitting on a pony. Then, one day during the summer, my family went to visit our cousins in the country. They own a big house and lots of land, and a stable. They keep four horses in it.

One of my cousins, Jerry, is the same age as me. He's always bragging about all sorts of things. If he's not bragging about his great school grades, he's bragging about what a great swimmer he is. If he's not boasting about his stamp collection, he's boasting about the big fish he caught last week. Well, this time, he began to boast about what a great horse rider he is. Then, he took me into the stable and showed me his very own pony!

"Nice, huh?" he said. "His name is Rusty!" He patted the horse on the rump. Rusty snorted. "Can *you* ride?"

"Oh, sure!" I lied. "I *love* to ride!"

"Well, then," said Jerry, "let's go for a ride around the ranch! Come on!"

Before I knew it, Jerry had saddled Rusty and the other pony, Hazel, and led them both out into the yard. They danced and pranced and snorted. I was afraid I'd get trampled.

"You said you love to ride," said Jerry. "Come on!"

He looked at me with his boasting eyes, then swung himself up on his pony.

"Well?" he said.

7

My family—my mother, father, I, my sister, and my brother—went camping in the woods often, but we had never gone so deep into the state forest before. As we drove through the thick woods, my dad said, "This time, everybody, we'll camp *away* from those scaredy-cat campers who are afraid of the wilderness! We're going where it's wild! There are bears in there, and deer and raccoons and even bobcats! This trip, we'll rough it!" he grinned.

We kids cheered and clapped. My mother just shook her head. "I hope it'll be safe in there!" she said.

"Don't worry!" said dad.

We drove deep into the woods, down bumpy dirt

roads. The trees grew tall and close together. We finally came to a large lake, and pitched our camp.

We put up our tents, built a campfire, and then cooked dinner—fish, fresh caught from the lake. It began to get dark as we put out the fire and cleaned up. It was time for bed. We all said good night to each other and crawled into our tents. (I had my own, because I'm the oldest.)

I couldn't fall asleep. For a long time, I just listened to the sounds of the forest. I also thought about what my father had said. Were there *really* bears and bobcats around? I shivered a little.

Finally, I began to fall asleep. Then, I heard a crack, like a twig snapping, right outside my tent. Then another *crack!* I sat up. What was *that?!!*

8

One sunny Sunday morning, my mother and father decided to take our family to the zoo. Were we excited! We all put on nice clothes. We packed a picnic lunch.

Although it was a very long car ride to the zoo, my brother and my sisters and I never noticed. We were busy chattering to each other about all the different animals we'd see, and which ones were our favorites.

In no time, it seemed, we arrived at the zoo. My father parked the car in the parking lot and we all got out, happy and laughing. "I want to see the monkeys!" my little brother cried.

Soon we were watching a keeper throw fish to the seals in the seal pond. They made funny noises—*ork! ork!*—and always caught the fish before it hit the water.

For a while we watched the monkeys in the monkey cage. We walked on and stopped to gaze at some African zebras, striped white and black, running around in a big, grassy field.

Soon, we came to the elephants. "Wow!" I said. The huge elephants were in a pen, surrounded by a low stone wall, and, with their long, thick trunks, they reached out to take peanuts and popcorn from people's hands. The trunks were pink on the ends, with two little holes.

"They breathe through these holes," said dad. "They use the trunks just like hands. Those tusks are really two big teeth!"

"Can we buy some peanuts for them?" asked my sister Doris.

"Sure!" said dad. He bought a big bag of peanuts from a vendor and gave each of us a handful. "Be careful!" dad said. "Those trunks are strong."

When an elephant picks a peanut from your hand, it tickles! We all laughed as we watched the big animals swing their trunks back and forth, then pop the peanuts into their mouths.

All of a sudden, Doris hollered, "Daddy, mommy, look!" She had moved in a little too close, and an elephant had reached out and snatched the straw hat right off her head! He swung it back and forth, high in the air!

9

Our teacher, Mrs. Marzipan, is one of the best and best-loved teachers in the school. She has been teaching third, fourth, and fifth grade classes for over eighteen years. Every child in the school knows her, not only because she's been here so long, and has taught the brothers and sisters of many of the children, but because she is a fine musician, too. She plays the piano at all the assemblies and important school events, such as the annual school play. She is a wonderful person, too. She makes you feel good about learning, and she never yells. She never *has* to yell. Children behave for her because they know that she appreciates good work and good behavior—you can tell. She loves to teach, and she loves children. That sounds corny, but that's what makes her such a terrific teacher.

Everyone in our class enjoyed Christmas vacation time, I'm sure. Christmas is a happy time—no school, no homework, no tests. Yet, we all missed Mrs. Marzipan. I know that as the vacation time was ending, I wanted it to go on and on, but at the same time I wanted to see Mrs. Marzipan so much!

The new term finally arrived. Many of us got to the schoolyard early, to compare notes. "What did you get for Christmas?" "You know what *I* got?" But when our principal, Mr. Amato, blew the whistle, we lined up quietly. Pretty soon, we thought, Mrs. Marzipan would be down to say hello!

We waited and waited. Where *was* she? All the other classes were going upstairs.

Mrs. Marzipan didn't come down.

Finally Mr. Amato came over to our line, accompanied by a man we had never seen before. The strange, neatly dressed young man must have been nervous. He kept twisting his fingers. He looked at us, then at Mr. Amato, then at us, over and over again. And he was carrying Mrs. Marzipan's keys!

"Children," said Mr. Amato, "I have something to tell you. Please listen! Mrs. Marzipan had an accident over the Christmas holiday and hurt her ankle. Until she comes back, your new teacher will be Mr. Ashton . . ."

10

Who likes to be cooped up in school when the weather is sunny and mild, just right for being outdoors and playing ball or flying a kite, or riding a bike? Not me! Neither did my friend in Mrs. Marshall's class. In my class I sat near the window, and my teacher, Mr. Vance, constantly reprimanded me for dreaming. I just couldn't keep my mind on the boring things he taught. He sounded, especially after lunch, like a 45 RPM record played at 33. The combination of nice weather and his droning voice made it hard for me to sit and listen and learn. So, sometimes my friend and I played hooky.

We didn't do it too often. Most of the time I was able to offer some fairly good excuse for my absence, and a couple of times, I handed in forged notes from my mother. I can imitate her handwriting pretty well. My friend wears thick glasses and always tells Mrs. Marshall that he had had an appointment with the eye doctor.

My mother was very worried about my schoolwork. She wanted me to go to college, to get someplace in life. She tried to talk to me, to put some sense into my head. I understood her perfectly well, but I never did follow her advice. When she worried, she smoked a lot, and she had trouble sleeping. Sometimes, I would find her at the kitchen table when I got up in the morning, piles of cigarette butts in the ashtray in front of her. She had blue circles under her eyes. I could feel her eyes follow me around the room as I fixed my breakfast.

"When are you going to straighten out?" she would ask me, not yelling, but in a caring, tired voice.

I couldn't answer her.

Last Wednesday, the weather was so beautiful, the temperature so mild, the sky such a pastel blue, that, on the way to school, my friend and I decided to play hooky. First we checked to see how much money we had between us. We had about nine dollars. We decided to spend the day at the amusement park!

The rides weren't running early in the morning, so we just walked around. After eleven o'clock, things began to open up. We played some games of chance and rode the roller coaster and ate hot dogs and french fries and corn on the cob. We had a great time! We rode on miniature stock car racers and we even went on the carousel. The music that the funny machine in the middle makes is just wonderful—when I get rich, I'm going to buy one of those machines and put it into my living room.

My friend and I ran out of money around two o'clock, so we went home. I got back to my house around half past three, the usual time. When I opened the front door, I was surprised to see my mother sitting in the living room, in the big armchair. She was smoking.

"Hello, Ma," I said, a little worried. "How come you're home from work so early?"

"Hello," she said in a flat voice. "How was school?"

"Oh," I said, "you know, the same as always." I tried to sound casual.

"Mr. Vance called me at work this afternoon," my mother said.

11

We were heading for the beach and rides, my kid brother and I. He was holding my hand so hard that it hurt. "Not so tight, kid," I had to say from time to time, because it got to be pretty uncomfortable. It was a pain having him hanging around me all the time. It seemed that whenever I wanted to have some fun with my friends, or by myself, there he'd be, following me around as if he were attached to me. And if I absolutely refused to have him with me, he'd bawl like a baby so that my mother would hear and come running. Then I'd *have* to take him with me, and I hated that.

Seeing the rides just ahead of us now, he perked up. He'd been quiet the whole time we were walking, but now he started asking me questions. Could we go on the roller coaster? Could we see the funny mirrors? Could we ride the carousel? Could we have ice cream? What a kid! He thought the world was there to feed him and show him a good time. He thought he had it coming to him. Of course, he was only six years old.

It was crowded inside the park. Children and their parents were everywhere, laughing, eating cotton candy, carrying balloons, fooling around. A man stood outside a big tent, talking into a microphone, telling everyone what a terrific time could be had inside. He spotted me and my brother. "Step right up!" he cried, his voice booming out at us through the loudspeakers. "Step right up, you two kids, for the greatest 25¢ show on earth!" We walked past the tent and stopped in front of a very skinny man with a big Adam's apple who, standing on a platform, was putting flaming rods into his mouth and pulling them out cold! He seemed to be eating the fire! My kid brother was fascinated. He stopped talking. His eyes opened wide. So did his mouth. I wasn't sure if *he* was scared, but I felt kind of afraid of the fire. My mouth had gone dry. So I said to him, "Look, kid, stay here a minute. I'm going to buy us a couple of sodas, okay?"

He didn't answer me. He was too absorbed by the fire-eater. So I left him there, with his mouth open, and made my way over to a nearby ice-cream wagon. I bought two cans of soda and worked my way back through the mob. I hadn't been gone more than five minutes, but when I got back to the fire-eater's platform again, I looked around and felt a tremendous sinking feeling in my stomach. *Where the heck was my kid brother?*

12

Ever since I can remember I had wanted a kitten or a puppy more than anything else in the world. Whenever I went anywhere with my parents, if we happened to pass by a pet shop window in which furry little things were frolicking and nipping at each other and tumbling around and around in the ripped-up pieces of newspaper, I would press my face to the glass and beg to go in. My parents had to pull me away. Whenever I met anyone with a puppy on a leash or with a little kitten, I wanted to stroke it and pet it and listen to the soft sounds it made. Oh, I really wanted a pet of my own! But every year, around Christmas or my birthday, when I asked for one my mom and dad would say, "You're not old enough to take care of a pet. When you're old enough, then we'll get you a puppy or a kitten." My dad would always add, "Of course you'll have to decide which kind you'd rather have." I spent hours thinking about how I'd take care of my pet and feed it and stroke it and love it in every way.

Several weeks ago, as my birthday approached, it was time to pop the question again. When my mom asked me, "What would you like for your birthday this year?" she and I both knew what my answer would be. This time my mom smiled a real big smile and said to me, "Your father and I have decided that you are now old enough to have a pet and take care of it."

"Wow!" I yelled. "Thanks, Mom!" I was so happy, I hugged her real tight. Then I ran outside to tell all my friends.

A week later my dad and mom and I went to the pet shop. There in the window was a little brown and white puppy. When I held out my hand he came right over and licked it and I knew he was the puppy I wanted for my very own! When we got home, I couldn't figure out what to call him, so my dad suggested a name. "How about Bowser?" he said. That sounded good to me. It seemed to fit. "Do you like your name, Bowser?" I asked him. He wagged his tail, so I knew he liked the name.

I really loved Bowser. He made little yipping noises and chewed on rags and towels. He sniffed around the whole house and followed me wherever I went. I made him a nice bed near the stove in a cardboard box. Next to the box was his water dish and food bowl.

I wanted to take Bowser around the neighborhood to show him to all my friends but my dad explained to me that Bowser was still too young to go outside. I invited some of the girls and boys in the neighborhood to come in and see him instead. They all thought he was a great looking puppy! Except Philip, who had two dogs of his own and didn't think there was anything special about Bowser. "That's just an ordinary dog!" Philip said. However, I didn't care what Philip said, because I loved Bowser and he was a special dog to me!

We fed Bowser only the best dog foods and some vitamin supplements, too, and he was a really healthy, active puppy. He still wasn't big enough to take out, not for another week or two, my dad said, but you could tell that Bowser wanted to know what was going on outside. He sometimes managed to get up on a window ledge by way of the back of one of the living room chairs, and from the ledge he'd look out into the street. He'd wait near the front door when he heard and smelled somebody coming and would stick his head out to see what was going on when the door was opened. My dad told me, "Always make sure when you leave the house, and even when you're in it, to put the snap on the door lock, because Bowser can push his way out, and until we start walking him around the neighborhood, he won't know the streets, and he could get lost." My dad really couldn't wait until Bowser was old enough to be taken for walks, because so far Bowser was only paper trained.

It was hot and stuffy in my room. I was on my bed, reading some comic books, and my little radio was playing some rock-'n'-roll music. Bowser was on the floor, knocking a rubber ball around with his paws, then pouncing on it. I was thirsty from the heat, but I was too lazy to get up to get a drink. When I thought about an ice cream pop, a nice cool ice cream pop, I got out of bed.

Bowser wanted to go along with me to the candy store. He whined as I closed the screen door behind me. "I'll be right back, Bowser," I said in a gentle voice. "I'll even let you lick a little off the stick, okay?"

"Woof?" said Bowser.

I ate most of the ice cream on the way back to the house, but I did save some for Bowser. As I walked up the front steps I called out, "Bowser!"

No answer. No barking.

"Bowser!" I called again. Where was he? Then I saw that the screen door wasn't locked. I had forgotten to snap it shut.

13

Last Thursday our teacher, Mrs. Robinson, announced, "On Monday, a new boy is coming into our class. His name is Douglas. I'm sure we're all going to make him feel welcome when he arrives."

Most of us listened to the announcement, since we usually act fairly civilized and listen to our teacher. *Most* of us, I said. The usual bunch of people paid no attention to what Mrs. Robinson said. Since she just seemed to mention the news in passing, as one of the daily items, like cookie sales and PTA meetings, most of us forgot about it in a few minutes. We went back to alphabetizing and breaking up our twenty spelling words into syllables.

Early Monday morning our principal, Mrs. Snyder, brought Douglas into the classroom. The class automatically became quiet, since that's what happens when a principal comes into a classroom. We looked at the new member of our class. He stared at the floor. As Mrs. Snyder spoke a few words in private to Mrs. Robinson, we stared at Douglas's very long, straight blond hair, his dungarees, his flannel shirt, and his scuffed shoes. He clutched a very worn and battered looseleaf notebook to his chest. We whispered to each other, "It's him, it's the new boy!" Someone, probably Ronald or Alan, said in a loud, rude voice, "Who's *that?*" and Mrs. Snyder turned her head and glared until whoever it was that had been so rude mumbled, "Sorry, Mrs. Snyder." The principal spoke for a few more minutes to our teacher, then left the room.

Mrs. Robinson introduced Douglas by saying, "This is the new member of our class, Douglas Hume." She smiled at him. He looked up for only a fraction of a second.

She sat him in the empty spot at table four, the place

John used to sit in before he moved to California six weeks ago. Nora and Helen and Troy didn't look too pleased to have him at their table. I really felt sorry for Douglas, because everyone was staring at him. You could tell that he was embarrassed to be the center of attention. Of course Mrs. Robinson soon had us working again, but we all looked across the room at Douglas every once in a while. He looked different. And so unhappy.

He *was* different. He was very quiet and spent most of the day staring down at his notebook, just straight down, not right, not left. Once in a while he shook his head to get the hair out of his eyes. He dressed strangely, we thought. No one in our class ever wore such bright plaid flannel shirts or dungarees that went all the way up in the front, like farmers' pants. We soon made up all sorts of stories about Douglas—that he was too poor to afford haircuts. That he never took baths. That he had come into the city right off the farm where he had milked cows and fed pigs, which was why he still wore his Farmer Joe pants. No one really tried to get to know him and find out anything truthful about him.

Wednesdays we are scheduled to have gym in the yard at two o'clock, and sometimes we get down there on time. Frequently we make such a racket lining up that Mrs. Robinson sits us down again. She won't take us out of the room until we're quiet.

Once we get downstairs, some of the girls take some jump ropes and some rubber balls and play over by the swings. The boys and five or six girls (including Nora and Helen, who can really sock that ball!) usually manage to form a punch-ball game. When I say usually, I mean that there is often so much shouting about who will play which position that Mrs. Robinson has to intervene. Which is what she had to do today. She got up from the bench (where she had been reading her newspaper) and announced, "All right, children, there are classes trying to work in the building. If you can't do this quietly, maybe we won't do it at all." She always says something like that. Then she said, as always, "I will pick the two captains. Russell and Henry, you choose your teams." She always picks those two as captains because they're the best players in the class and ought to be on opposite sides in a game, she says.

Mrs. Robinson watched the children choose sides. Douglas stood about ten feet away from the group, observing, shaking his long hair from his eyes. He was, of course, the last one to be chosen. He turned out to be Russell's pick.

"Do I have to choose him?" asked Russell. "I don't think he knows how to play ball!"

"Yes," said Mrs. Robinson, firmly.

"Okay," said Russell, and he gestured to Douglas. He put him up last, and made him the catcher so he couldn't drop any ball in the outfield. Douglas didn't say anything. He just looked sad and nervous.

Well, punch-ball games are almost always high-scoring games, and Russell's team, which batted first (they won the toss of one of Mrs. Robinson's nickels) socked balls all over the yard. In less than three minutes, they had five runs. There were two out, men and women (Troy and Helen) on first and third. Russell was jumping around and yelling, "Let's keep the rally going! Who's up? Let's keep it going! Who's up?"

It was Douglas's turn to hit.

He stepped up to the plate, looking scared and shy. "I'll bet he can't hit it five feet," I heard Henry say to Billy in the outfield. They moved in. Even Mrs. Robinson stood up to watch Douglas. He bounced the ball on the plate four times . . .

14

Our tribe of several thousand Indians lived on the southern portion of the long narrow island. We called it *Manhatta*, which means "hilly" in our language. Life was good for our tribe. Most of the time we led a very peaceful life. We fished in the clean river and in the sparkling streams for sturgeon, perch, trout, and striped bass. Sometimes we fished from shore, and sometimes from our canoes which we made from the trunks of huge trees that grew on our land. In the forests we hunted for deer, bear, and squirrel. We trapped mink and beaver in the marshes and used the furs to keep us warm in the winter. In the summer we wore very little except a coating of bear grease which kept the flies and mosquitoes from biting and protected our skin from the sun. The women gathered blueberries and wild cherries from the woods and tended the vegetable gardens. We made our huts out of pieces of tree bark fastened together, with a hole in the middle of the roof to let the smoke from the fire escape. This sort of chimney didn't work too well, but at least, in the smoke-filled huts, the mosquitoes didn't bother us too much. There was plenty of marsh and swampland on the island, and in spring and summer the insects came out in swarms!

One June morning my brothers and I were checking our muskrat traps on the eastern shore of the island when one of our friends, Shorakin, came splashing through the shallow marsh to where we were examining our lines. He was out of breath.

"Come! Come!" he panted. "Big boats are in the river!" His greased skin glistened in the sun.

He was very excited. We hung the few animals we had trapped in a tall bush, to keep them out of the mouths of the wolves and wild dogs, and hurried after him. About a third of the mile down a trail through tall marsh grass, we made a left turn and were soon standing on the river shore.

Many braves had gathered to watch. Some held spears, some carried bows and arrows, for they had been hunting in the forest when the word spread. With them were the women holding their babies, and small children clutching their mothers' legs.

My brothers and I gazed with wonder at the big ships in the river, just as the others did. We had never seen boats so large, nor so strange. Tall trees sprouted from these boats, and great white animal skins hung from their trunks instead of leaves. One of the boats had hollow logs sticking out of its sides.

We were not afraid, as I said, merely curious. As we stood and watched, a small wooden boat was let down the side of one of the big boats, and when this was in the water four men climbed down ropes and got into this small boat. Then they began to paddle to shore, toward us! One of the men was waving what looked like a colorful piece of animal skin attached to a long thin stick.

Suddenly we heard a tremendous noise: *Boom!* and a white cloud appeared from one of the hollow logs! An enormous round stone flew through the air and crashed into a big tree and smashed its trunk! Women screamed, children cried. As the crown of the tree smashed and tore its way down to the ground, many turned and ran into the woods. My brother and I and Shorakin, frightened, hid behind trees and rocks and watched the small boat come closer and closer.

15

They don't sell baseball cards the same way today as they did when I was your age. Back then in the Five and Ten Cent Store you could buy three packs packaged together with cellophane, and no bubble gum, for only ten cents. When you bought them in the candy store, you got five cards for a nickel, and a piece of gum nobody ever chewed because it was usually stale. Seems like a million years ago. The only thing wrong with the bargain was that the cards in the cellophane packages only went up to number 125 or so, which meant that about three-fourths of the cards in the set of 500 were not available at the low price.

I must have been about eight years old when I first got interested in baseball. All the other girls and boys on the block were collecting baseball cards. I didn't get much of an allowance (if I remember correctly, it was about fifteen cents a week) and when the kids on my block, like Felix and Janey and Kevin and all the others, swapped cards and flipped them and pitched them against the wall, I never had very many cards to play with. Which is why, I guess, I started to slick them from the Five and Ten. The first time I stole some, my heart really pounded until I got out of the store and ran, but it was much easier to do the next time. Pretty soon I had a nice thick pile of cards to do things with. Of course, I had about ten trillion duplicates, since I didn't have many cards higher than number 125. I had about nineteen Andy Careys (he used to play third base for the Yankees) and at least twenty-five Chuck Hintons. I think he was an outfielder for the Dodgers. I'd have to look it up to be sure.

One afternoon I was sitting on the curbstone in front of my apartment building waiting for Joe, the Good Humor Ice Cream man, to come along in his truck. Felix and Janey came along the street and sat down next to me. They both lived in the brownstone houses down the block, right next door to each other and they were good friends, most of the time. They were such good friends that sometimes they'd look at each other and you knew that they had all sorts of secrets they never shared with anyone else. They sat down on the curb, as I said, one on each side of me, and looked at me.

"Hi," I said.

Janey said, "We know something about you."

Felix said, "Yeah."

Janey said, "We know where you get all those baseball cards!"

Felix said, "Yeah, we know!"

I got scared. "No you don't," I said. I hadn't told *anybody* where they came from.

"You better give us your ice cream money or we'll go up and tell your mother!" said Felix. He looked at me, then across me at Janey.

I was worried. I didn't want my mother and father to find out that I was stealing. I stood up. "You don't know anything!" I said.

"Give us ten cents," said Felix, "or we'll tell!"

I was terrified! I threw two nickels on the ground and ran into my house and up the stairs. Felix and Janey picked up the money, then ran after me, into the apartment building.

"We're gonna te-ell! We're gonna te-ell!" Janey chanted. I had to stop for breath at the third-floor landing. I heard Felix ask, "Where does he live?" Then I took off again.

My mother was preparing supper. When I burst into the house and slammed the door she almost dropped a pot of vegetables.

"What's the matter?" she yelled. "Did you run up the stairs?"

"Yeah," I panted. I lied: "I got to go to the bathroom."

"Then go!" she said. "And get out of here till supper time! And stay clean!"

"Yeah," I said. I put my ear to the front door. I didn't hear any noise in the hallway. I hoped Janey and Felix had gone outside again. I went to the front window and peeked out. They were not in front of the house. I didn't see them downstairs.

"Are you still here?" my mom yelled. "Will you get downstairs?" She looked at me. "What's the matter with you today?" she asked me. "Why are you creeping around like that?"

Before I could think of an answer, the doorbell rang three times. *Ring! Ring! Ring!*

16

I was born under a big, overhanging rock, behind some sweet-scented red cypress trees, and my earliest memory is of being licked from head to toe by my mother. I was standing on my wobbly, spindly legs, and she was cleaning bits of old leaves and cypress needles and soil from my soft, wet coat. It was very early in the morning and in the forest birds whistled and flew and yellow dapples of sunlight were everywhere.

When my legs were strong enough to support me without wobbling, my mother and I carefully picked our way through the forest in search of tender leaves and grasses to eat. Then we made our way down the mountain to the stream, to drink. We often met other does there, with fawns as young as I. The bucks stayed off by themselves, in the woods. During the day, mother and I usually stayed close to the big rock and the protective red cypresses. We moved about more freely at dusk and at night. It was safest then, because we knew that the hunters came during the day. They couldn't see well at night, as we deer could.

We had many enemies in the forest. My mother taught me about them—bears, wildcats, and wolves. I quickly learned to freeze the instant I heard suspicious noises. My skin, like all young deer's, was spotted white, yellow, and brown, and when I stood still, I blended into the bushes.

I learned to use my nose, too. My mother taught me to recognize the smells of wolf and bear, and to recognize their tracks. And, of course, as my legs got stronger I learned to run and jump. I was soon leaping over bushes taller than myself. It was fun!

My mother taught me about the hunters, too. They were more dangerous to us than the wolves, for they had weapons that could shoot an animal from one hundred feet away! And, unlike wolves and wildcats, they did not hunt only when they were hungry. They would hunt as many animals as they could, and save the meat to eat during the winter. They used animal skins as clothing and they sometimes put the antlers of the bucks on the walls of their cabins. They were very dangerous, my mother taught me, and whenever we came across their tracks or their scent in the woods we ran and leaped away as fast as we could.

Summer came and I grew quickly. It was not long before I was big enough and strong enough to go off into the woods by myself for hours at a time, and I returned to the big rock and to my mother during the hottest part of the day, to sleep or rest. Many of the spots were gone from my coat.

I hadn't seen any hunters for several months. My mother told me that they didn't hunt when the weather was warm. So, I forgot some of the things I had learned. There were very few hunters and hunter scents around to remind me to be careful.

One evening just as the sun dipped behind the mountains, I joined a group of other deer, mothers and youngsters, and went down the mountain to drink in the stream. One of the oldest does led the way; she had the best hearing, and every few feet she stopped and her ears and nose twitched as she examined sounds and smells from all over the mountainside. My friends and I were not as careful. We bounded down the grassy slopes on the soft pads of our feet.

Soon we reached the stream. A young buck stepped into the cool water and bent his head down to drink. I stepped carefully on the mossy rocks. It was silent and warm and quiet, except for a few buzzing flies. Suddenly I heard a whistling sound. A young buck standing nearby snorted and then cried out. *Bang!* A shot rang through the wood and hit a tree trunk just inches above the buck's head! A hunter came out of the bushes! Another came from behind a tree! I slipped on a mossy stone and . . .

17

My birthday was only two weeks away.

Most kids feel really excited as their birthdays approach. They think about the party, the presents, the balloons, the games, the cake with the candles, and how they'll become a really important person for a day—a person so important that people they hardly ever see during the year, and relatives they hardly ever think about, send presents and cards, some with a little money folded inside.

However, I was puzzled. My birthday was only two weeks away and my mother hadn't said anything to me yet about a party. I thought to myself, "It takes time to plan birthday parties. You have to plan weeks in advance. So why hasn't mom said anything about mine? And why hasn't she asked me what I'd like to have for a present?"

I was so puzzled that I went into the kitchen to talk to my mom.

She was peeling potatoes to go with the roast beef she was cooking for dinner that evening. She didn't stop peeling as I asked her, "Mom, am I having a birthday party this year?"

My mother smiled, almost to herself. She didn't even look at me.

"My, you're growing up, aren't you?" she said.

"That didn't answer my question, Mom!" I insisted.

"There's a lot of time between now and then," she said. "Now, go out and play. Come back in an hour for supper."

I went outside.

After dinner, my dad settled into his armchair in the den to read the sports pages. He had a bottle of beer on the little table next to him. I approached him.

"Hi, there," said dad. "How come you picked at your food tonight? That was good roast beef. It costs plenty of money a pound."

"I wasn't too hungry," I answered. I paused. "Daddy, has mom said anything to you about a birthday party for me? I mean, which relatives and friends will be there, and everything?"

"Oh, that's right! Your birthday is coming up soon!" said dad. "I had forgotten. As for your question, you know that your mother handles things like that. Why don't you ask her?"

Crestfallen, I replied, "Okay, Daddy, I'll ask her." I left the den, went outside, and sat down on the front porch. I was very puzzled.

Louis, the neighborhood genius, happened to be walking down the street at that moment, whistling. When he saw me sitting with my head in my hands, he came over to me.

"What's the matter?" asked Louis.

"Hi, Louis," I said. "Say, they don't call you the neighborhood genius for nothing. Maybe you can figure out what's going on, or tell me what to do."

"Why not?" said Louis, modestly. He sat down next to me. Louis was the sort of boy who, if you saw him, would immediately make you think: there's an intelligent-looking young fellow! He looked smart. He always carried a book. Tonight he was carrying *A Child's Guide to Modern American Literature*.

I told Louis what was puzzling me. It didn't take him long to come up with a few suggestions.

Louis said, "Listen. You know your parents wouldn't

forget to throw you a party, right? You know they are not going to forget to give you presents. It seems to me that this year, they are going to give you a *surprise* birthday party! Otherwise, why would they be so wishy-washy about the subject when you bring it up?"

"Maybe you're right," I said.

"Not only that, but it may not even be in your house. They may not want you to find the decorations and presents and things, if you snoop around for them. So the party, if it *is* a surprise party, will therefore be held in your Uncle Jerry's house *around the corner!*"

I jumped up. "You're a genius!" I cried. "Thanks, Louis!"

"Nothing to it," said Louis. "It all comes natural to me." He said good-bye to me, then continued on down the street, whistling classical tunes, as geniuses often do.

The days passed and my birthday drew nearer and nearer. I snooped around the house, when my mom was out shopping, and found no party decorations, no balloons, no bags of candy stuck away—although, of course, these were things that could always be purchased at the last minute. I didn't find any present hidden about, either. My mom and dad said nothing about a party, nor did they ask me what I wanted for my birthday. It sure seemed as if they intended to surprise me! I wondered what they'd get me. A new bike?

Birthday morning! I was up with the sun. I hadn't slept much during the night. I was too excited.

I rushed into the kitchen and made myself a nice breakfast of Rice Krispies and banana slices, and gobbled it down. A few minutes later, my parents came into the kitchen. Dad was dressed for work. My mother wore her blue bathrobe.

"Morning," I said. I looked carefully at my parents' faces. Did they look as if they were keeping a secret?

"Did you use up all the milk?" asked Mom. "I can't find it."

"It's way in the back," I said. I watched my parents eat breakfast. My mother was quiet and thoughtful. She put down her coffee cup and said, "Oh, by the way, this is very important. Uncle Jerry and Aunt May want you to drop by this afternoon around five o'clock. Don't be early, they won't be home. Okay?"

"Okay!" I said. "I'll be there, all right!"

18

We used to live on the second floor of an apartment building on Grant Avenue. Our windows faced the front (which was considered really great; if your windows didn't face front, you sometimes had a view of the alley or wash hanging on lines to dry). Right next door to us lived Mrs. Stone, the nosiest lady in the whole neighborhood.

Her husband worked in the post office and dragged himself home every evening about five o'clock. Nobody ever saw him until the next morning. But everybody saw Mrs. Stone, all day long, because all day long she leaned on her dirty yellow pillow on her windowsill and watched everything that happened in the street below. Sometimes, you could feel her funny little round black eyes follow you around. Not only her eyes were funny, either. She was about the skinniest lady you could ever possibly meet. Her head swayed on top of her skinny neck like a tulip in the breeze.

And was she nosey! My mother didn't have time to lean out windows and watch the world go by down on Grant Avenue. She had to take care of my two squawky little brothers and my sisters and me. That kept her busy, all that cooking and cleaning and shopping and ironing, but she knew what I was up to all the time. Mrs. Stone kept her up to date. Since I wasn't permitted to cross the street or leave the block, it was easy for Mrs. Stone to watch every move I made and report it to my mom. I would come up for a glass of milk and my mom would say to me, "Were you fooling around with Mr. Cooper's dog again? Mrs. Stone told me she saw you playing with it!" Or, when I came up for supper, my mom might say, "I heard you were playing with Vincent and Jeannie again! I told you not to play with them! They're not nice children to play with!" Mrs. Stone was my mom's X-ray eyes. Sometimes, I wondered if my mom paid her for spying on me. Probably not. She liked to do it. She did it for nothing.

A lot of times it was hard to have fun playing outside. I felt like every move I made was being spied on. It seemed like every time I looked up at Mrs. Stone's window, she was staring at me. All the other boys and girls on the block thought she was funny, too; they never remembered her name, just her skinny arms hanging out the windows, so down on the street we called her Bones.

One summer afternoon she left her window at about one-thirty to get her lunch, which she always ate while leaning on the sill, and didn't come back. I wondered about that for a few minutes, then forgot about her. Kevin and Shirley and Janey and Paul were organizing a game of tag. They made me "it." They got a ten second lead on me, then I was supposed to run after them and throw a rubber ball and try to hit somebody with it. If I hit somebody, he or she became "it."

Well, they scattered. I counted to ten and started after them, but I slowed down when I saw where they were going—they were running down the cellar steps! I wasn't allowed to go down there, and I hesitated. I looked up at Mrs. Stone's window—she wasn't there! *Zoom!* I took off down the cellar steps after my friends.

The cellar was dark and there were a lot of twists and turns and funny corners. I was scared, but as long as I kept going, I didn't feel *too* scared. I passed garbage cans, fuse boxes, old baby carriages coated with dust. A strange yellow light seeped down from the high, dusty windows. Where *were* they? Footsteps. Cries. Waterpipes, cobwebs. I thought I saw something up ahead. I raised my arm and got ready to throw the ball. I was running out of breath. "Gotcha!" I shouted and threw the ball at the first body I saw as I turned the next corner.

"Aah!" cried Mrs. Stone. The ball hit her smack in the stomach and she fell right on her behind! Her laundry scattered all over the place and a cup of bleach splashed all over the dirty floor!

19

A new girl came into Ed's class a few days after Thanksgiving, and he fell in love with her right away. Her name was Cindy. She was little and thin, so thin that the bones in her arms seemed no thicker than pencils. She had dark brown, really curly, kinky hair, and a long nose. Ed fell in love with her the moment he saw her. Perhaps it was her eyes. She had really clear blue eyes, the color of the blue marbles you get when you buy a bag from the dime store. But most of all, as Ed looked at her from across the room (Miss Kranedas sat her at table four, in the front of the room near the door), he saw that she was shy and afraid of all the strange kids in the class, and he knew exactly how she felt. He was kind of shy himself, so he didn't open his mouth too much in class, or make a lot of noise and bother people.

When some people fall in love, they stop acting the way they ordinarily do. They stop working, look dreamy, stare into space, sigh, or look starry-eyed. Ed didn't get like that. Nobody noticed that he had fallen in love with Cindy and he didn't tell anyone, not even his best friend Felix. Felix teased him a lot even though he was his best friend. The other children in the class sometimes made fun of Ed because of his shyness, and because he wasn't too good at sports, and because he always did his work and Miss Kranedas was always complimenting him and giving him extra cookies at snack time. They called Ed "Teacher's Pet" and other names. So, of course, he didn't want any of the big mouths in the class like Ronald and Glenn to know how he felt about Cindy. And, he was too shy to tell Cindy how he felt about her.

So, he wrote little notes to her and sent her little presents. He wrote poems on pieces of assignment book paper. One read,

> *In summer it's warm, in winter it's ice,*
> *I think you are very, very nice.*
>   —Anonymous.

He signed every note and poem, "Anonymous." He folded

each one up very carefully and snuck them into her coat pocket. Luckily, in his classroom, the girls and boys used the same cloak room. Ed was very careful. No one noticed. He wrapped little toys and Cracker Jacks prizes and slipped them into her pockets, too. He sent Cindy a toy or note almost every day. Then he'd return to his seat and wait to see how she'd react when she read the note or opened the little package. She didn't show them to anyone else, because she kept to herself and wasn't too friendly with any of the other girls yet, even the girls at her own table. She seemed pleased to get the little notes and the presents. She'd look around and wonder who could have sent them. Once, Ed thought he saw her blush as she read one of his poems, but it was hard to tell for sure from all the way across the room.

Cindy never got to keep the little green plastic fish Ed sent her. Miss Kranedas happened to be passing by the very moment she unwrapped it. The teacher looked down and said, "What is that nonsense?" She took the fish away. Then she read the note the fish had been wrapped in to the class. "My goodness!" she said. "Cindy, you have a very generous admirer in the room!"

> *You are so swell, it makes me want to yell.*
> *I think you are neat and really sweet.*
> —Anonymous

The class laughed. Cindy smiled shyly.

Miss Kranedas looked around the room. "Which one of you imps sent this?" she asked. In a million years, no one would have suspected Ed. She stared at Ronald.

"It wasn't me!" he said in a loud voice. "I hate girls!"

Ed didn't write any notes to Cindy for two weeks. Finally, he decided to write her a poem.

He waited until recess time. The school had a big schoolyard, and Ed sat in the shade of a big oak tree, by himself. There was no snow on the ground, even though it was February, so the class had gone outdoors to play. Most of the boys and a few girls were over on the other side of the yard, playing a noisy game of kickball. The rest of the girls were playing jump rope. Ed could see Cindy turning the rope, and chanting along with the rest of the girls, but he couldn't hear the words of the chant. He was too far away.

So far he had written,

> *Dear Cindy,*
> *Because you are shy, and so am I*
> *I like you so much, my heart's in the sky*

Ed held the paper out and read the words to himself. Pretty good, so far! he thought. He looked up and across the yard at Cindy again for a moment, and his heart thumped. He sighed. He was just about to write another line when Ronald and Glenn, who had been hiding behind the tree, jumped out! Glenn grabbed the paper from Ed's hand and ran, yelling, with Ronald close behind, across the yard to the other kids.

20

Last year I was in the same class as Patricia. You know who I mean, the *famous* Patricia, the kid who always gets in so much trouble. That's right, the one whose mother thinks she's an angel and that her teacher is always picking on her. Everybody knows about her. She's famous. Last year we were in the same class, and, for a while, at the same table.

No one could figure out what was the matter with her. She looked unhappy all the time. She always came in late in the mornings, complaining that she hadn't eaten any breakfast and that she couldn't do her work because she was so hungry. She was never prepared, either. Even when Mrs. Marzipan gave her a paper and pencil to work with she hardly ever did anything. She'd draw pictures for a while, on the paper and on her table, or scribble, or make an airplane out of the worksheet. She was always bringing toys and games and dolls and other stuff into school, too. She constantly called out, shouted insults, stood on her chair or table, was the first one to the door when someone knocked, even though she sat all the way over on the other side of the room. (She was as far away from Mrs. Marzipan as she could be, and I think the teacher liked it that way.) She was very fresh and talked back to our teacher and to our principal, Mr. Vonz. They didn't know what to do about Patricia. Every time they called her mother into school, Patricia's mother made such a fuss and was so unreasonable, they just gave up. The other kids were bothering her Patricia, she insisted. Patricia was a good girl.

Patricia also liked to use her hands—she would punch and pinch the other children even when Mrs. Marzipan was looking, if she didn't get things her own way. If she didn't get what she wanted immediately, whether it was permission to go to the bathroom, or to get a drink of water, or to sharpen a pencil (on the rare occasions when she had one), or to play with her toys, or to work as a monitor in the office, or to look at some other pupil's book, or comic, she made a fuss, threw a tantrum, hit and yelled and pinched.

She never bothered *me* very much. Even though we sat at the same table, I managed to ignore her and do my work. Plus, I am a few inches taller than Patricia, and heavier. She never bothered me. She sometimes said ridiculous things, but I could tell by the way she said the words that she was bluffing. She never looked me in the eye when she said them. That's how I could tell.

One afternoon, right in the middle of a math lesson, as Mrs. Marzipan was getting a little frazzled because some of us weren't picking up the lesson too well, a funny thing happened. Patricia hadn't been paying any attention. Instead, she had been making noises with her tongue and lips, and we all had been ignoring her. Suddenly, she got up from her seat, walked to the clothing closet, took a bag of potato chips from her coat pocket, sat down, and began to eat them, *crunch, crunch, crunch!*

Mrs. Marzipan blew up! Not only is it against her room regulations to eat in class, she always gets extremely angry when someone is rude enough to ignore her when she is teaching something new. Except for Patricia, of course. But the potato chips did it and Mrs. Marzipan blew her top!

"Where is your pencil?" she yelled as she stomped over to Patricia's seat. She grabbed the bag of chips from her hand. Was she furious! Her face was turning red!

"I ain't got one!" Patricia answered in nasty voice. "I lost it!"

"Where's your book? Why isn't it out? How can you do your math if your book isn't even out?!"

"I left it at home."

"Where is your pencil?" Mrs. Marzipan yelled again, as if she hadn't heard the answer to her first question.

"I got one right here!" Patricia sneered. To my astonishment, she took from her desk one of *my* pencils, imprinted in gold with my name!

"Hey!" I said, "that's mine!" I stood up and tried to grab the pencil from Patricia's hand.

"What are you doing with that pencil?" shouted Mrs. Marzipan. She was as red in the face as a beet. "That's it! That's it! Get down to the office! Get out! I'm getting you suspended! *Get out!*"

Patricia shoved her chair out violently, got up, and marched to the door. In the doorway, she turned and looked at me.

"I'll get you!" she called. "You got me in trouble!" She left.

The class was very quiet. Mrs. Marzipan sat down at her desk and put her head into her hands.

Patricia was out of the room for the rest of the day. We more or less forgot about her for a while. It was almost peaceful in the room for the rest of the afternoon.

After Mrs. Marzipan dismissed us at three o'clock, I hung around in front of the school for a few minutes and talked to a couple of my friends. Then I started home. Just as I passed the alley next to the A & P I heard a voice calling me.

"Hey, you!"

I turned my head. There stood Patricia, clenching her fists.

"You got me into trouble!"

21

When I was very young my family lived in an old apartment building that had been constructed over fifty years ago. It didn't have an elevator or an incinerator chute, so when a family had to get rid of its garbage, somebody had to take it down to the cellar and place it in a can. Of course, in some places people toss trash bags out the windows, into backyards or into alleys, but my neighborhood was a nice one in those days and no one did things like that. Luckily, my family lived on the second floor, so it wasn't much of a bother to walk down to the basement with the garbage. The people who lived on the upper floors had to walk a long way.

After I grew big enough and smart enough my mom used to send me down with the trash, but I didn't like to go. You see, we had a strange superintendent in our building. Her name was Josie, and she frightened me. Almost all the kids in the building and on the whole block were scared of her and her big brown and white dog, Sheppie.

She was a good super. She never let us play in the courtyard, or in the trees in the yard. We weren't permitted to play on the cellar steps, or to bounce a ball in the hallway. Oh, you could get away with it for a few minutes, if you were brave, but sooner or later, and usually pretty soon, Josie would hear the noise and come out of her dark little apartment in the cellar, dragging Sheppie on a leash. She just seemed to *appear*. She probably wore soft shoes or slippers, or maybe no shoes at all. You never heard her coming. She just *appeared!* And what an appearance! We kids would run when we saw her and her big barking dog (who, by the way, never bit anybody). She was a short, stout woman who wore old print dresses and kerchiefs. She couldn't move fast because she had some sort of trouble with her legs and her ankles were always fat and swollen. Even before they became fashionable, she wore rimless glasses, and her eyes, the color of Seven-Up bottle glass, just seemed to bore right through you as she said in her flat voice, "Get away with the ball in the court. No playing with the ball in the court." Her English wasn't perfect (I think my mom once told me that Josie had come from Yugoslavia many years ago) but you always got the message. If for some reason you didn't, she would, no matter what floor you lived on, soon appear at your door to tell your mom or dad what you had done. The mothers and fathers listened to every word she said. She never lied. She was a good super. Despite her bad legs and slow speed she kept the building neat and clean and nice.

I mentioned that I did not like to go down with the garbage. I didn't mind the smell, and I didn't mind the work. I was just afraid that I'd run into Josie and Sheppie in the shadowy, scary basement. The garbage cans were kept in the cellar during most of the day and at night. The sanitation men came early in the morning to empty the cans. Josie had a helper, Otto, who took them up to the street and down for her when they were empty. I once asked my mom, "How come Josie doesn't leave the cans on the street, so they don't have to be carried up and down all the time?" She answered, "It keeps the sidewalk in front of the house neater."

Late one summer evening my mom said to me, "Will you please take down these two bags of refuse? I don't want them in the kitchen. They'll start to smell and attract roaches. It's hot in the kitchen."

I made a face, but I said, "Okay, Mom." I picked up

the two bags and went downstairs. I paused at the top of the cellar stairs, then picked my way carefully down. Not only did I not want to stumble in the dark, I did not want to make a single sound.

The cellar door was open, but because I was carrying two big bags of garbage I couldn't see where I was putting my feet. In the dimness, I stumbled over a loose metal drain cover, and fell. The bags broke and the garbage scattered all over! What was worse, I had bumped the door with my shoulder and now it swung shut with a *Boom!* and a click, cutting off almost all the light except for what came in from the streetlights through the high dusty windows. I tried to stand up. I heard a creaking noise behind me. I turned my head and, frozen to the spot, I watched Josie's apartment door slowly open!

22

My mother's birthday was coming up, and I wanted to get her something nice. I didn't know what, just something nice, because she was a good mom. She kept her temper even though I got on her nerves a lot. She only punished me when I deserved to be punished, which is pretty fair, you have to admit; and she cooked good meals for our family. She was a good mom, and I wanted to get her something really nice.

I kept my money hidden in the back of my closet in an old jam jar, wrapped in a sock, inside a jigsaw puzzle box (half the pieces of which had been thrown out the window by my little brother). I dug it out and took the sock off, unscrewed the lid, and poured all the money out on my bed. I counted all the nickels and dimes and pennies and quarters three times and I came up with the same total each time: one dollar and seventeen cents! One measly dollar and seventeen cents! I thought I had a lot more than that! Peanuts! What sort of gift could I get with that, and my mom's birthday only six days away?

I put the money back in the jar and hid it in the closet. For a few moments I wondered if my little brother had come across the jar and had thrown some of my money out the window (he was too little to need or understand what money was), but I quickly dismissed the possibility. He was afraid of deep, dark closets. I sat down on my bed and tried to think of something to do. I needed some money!

Just then my mother poked her head in the room to see what I was up to. She observed that I wasn't up to any mischief, then said, "You know, your Uncle Nathan is coming for dinner tonight." She left.

I jumped up and whirled around. The answer to my problem! Rich old Uncle Nathan! He was sure to slip me a few bucks after dinner, like he almost always did! He would solve my problem! Then I sobered up and sat down again. Uncle Nathan was strange in certain ways. He was just as likely to slip me ten cents as ten dollars. And once, he had given me a coupon he had clipped from a newspaper, good for seven cents off on a bottle of dandruff shampoo. You never knew what he would do. Well, I thought to myself, maybe he'll be in a generous mood after the meal. I hope my mom cooks a really great dinner.

Uncle Nathan was a *different* sort of person. He never bothered about what other people, including, of course, the people in our family, thought about how he lived his life or acted or dressed (which is an advantage, I guess, to having a lot of money—you don't have to worry about things like that). As I sat at dinner that night, kicking my brother back every time he kicked me under the table, I looked at Uncle Nathan, with his curly white hair, red face, and long, thin nose. He wore an old-looking dark grey suit and a red shirt, buttoned all the way up to the neck, with no tie, and blue suspenders. On the lapel of his jacket he wore a little brass button he had gotten when he worked in an airplane factory during World War I. He was very proud of it. He always wore it. I once asked my mother if Uncle Nathan transferred that button to his pajamas when he went to sleep and she replied, smiling, "He probably has another one that he wears on his pajamas."

We had a nice dinner, roast beef that my mom always cooks just the right way. My little brother didn't throw any vegetables around (I think my dad had a talk with him before the meal), and after dessert we all went into the living room and sat down and looked at each other.

My parents and Uncle Nathan talked for a while. Finally Uncle Nathan said, "Well, it's getting late." He took out a cigar, but didn't offer my dad one. Once he had offered one to *me*.

"I have to get to bed early tonight, but I brought you each a little something you can use," said Uncle Nathan. "Harriet, I loved the meal, except the napkins scratched my lips. You must try a softer brand. Here's something for you." From a pocket in his jacket he took out a china salt shaker. It was shaped like a mushroom.

"Oh, thank you, Uncle Nathan, it's lovely!" cried my mother.

"And for you, Joe!" Uncle Nathan said to my father as

he pulled a pepper shaker from another pocket. It looked just like the salt shaker, except that it had a little green frog sitting on top.

My dad said, "Very nice item, Uncle Nathan, thanks."

My little brother Billy had been fidgeting. Uncle Nathan looked at him and smiled. "Little boy," he said, "I've got something very special for you!" My brother was in Uncle Nathan's lap before he finished his sentence. "Look!"

Billy's gift was a rubber monkey on the end of a tube. It hopped and jumped every time you squeezed a little rubber bulb. Billy squealed with delight.

Meanwhile, I was wondering what Uncle Nathan was going to give *me*. Oh, I hoped it would be at least a dollar. I wanted to get a nice gift for my mom. I tried to beam my thoughts into Uncle Nathan's head. At last, he turned to me and said, "And for you, child, come over here and see what I've got for *you!*"

He puffed on his cigar. I walked over as he reached into his pocket.

23

Our neighborhood used to be so safe, you didn't even have to lock your door when you left your house. You didn't have to lock your car doors, either, and you could leave all sorts of stuff on the front porch over night. You didn't have to worry about coming home from somewhere very late at night and, during the summer, the people who lived in the three-story apartment buildings nearby sat outside on beach chairs until twelve or one o'clock in the morning. My friend Larry's mother used to prop open the door to their apartment with a chair to let a breeze in the house. Everyone felt safe and secure in our neighborhood.

Things couldn't stay that way forever, I suppose.

One morning Mrs. Robbins came over to our house while my mother was fixing breakfast for my little sister and me. Mrs. Robbins looked a little puzzled.

"Good morning, Mary," said my mom. "Something the matter?"

"Morning," said Mrs. Robbins. She nodded to my sister and me. We were halfway through our bowls of Cheerios. My sister had most of hers all over her face and dripping down her chin.

"Yes, there is," said Mrs. Robbins. "I can't find my portable radio. I thought I left it on the back porch last night. I'm sure I remember leaving it there when Jim and I went in, but it wasn't there this morning and I looked all over and I just don't know where it could be."

"Well," said Mom, "you probably just misplaced it and I'm sure it'll turn up."

"I certainly hope so," said Mrs. Robbins. "I just put new batteries in it, too."

That was just the beginning. Things started to disappear from porches and patios. Radios, lemonade pitchers, baseball gloves, and, finally, someone's bicycle. Obviously, there was a thief around. For the first time, people locked their doors at night and left nothing outside.

"No sense tempting a thief with anything," was what the neighbors said to one another. Folks became suspicious of strangers and watched carefully any unfamiliar person they saw in the neighborhood.

About a week later, thieves broke into the Watson house at around two o'clock in the morning. That's what time the police figured they broke in, because they found an unplugged clock radio, stopped at two o'clock, and guessed that the thieves had meant to take the clock along, then forgotten it. Somehow they had known that the Watsons were away.

"Hey, Dad," I asked the next day. "How the heck did they get away with a TV and all that other stuff and nobody heard them or saw them? How'd they get that stereo out? That was a big stereo!"

"Thieves are clever," said my dad, "and I think we are going to get new locks put on our doors."

My mother was worried. She said, "What would have happened if the Watsons had been home? Suppose they had surprised the crooks?"

"The thieves wouldn't have broken in if they knew somebody was home," answered my dad. "Stop worrying."

"Nobody's going to steal anything out of this house if I can help it!" I announced. From that night on, I kept one of my dad's old golf clubs next to my bed at night, just in case.

Things quieted down in the neighborhood for a while after the burglary at the Watsons'. People made sure their doors and windows were locked. But then one night, I couldn't sleep. The mosquitoes were bothering me, even though we had screens in our windows, and I sat up in bed in the dark and scratched my left arm.

What was that?

I thought I heard a thumping noise coming from downstairs. The house was very quiet, except for my father's snoring, which I could hear through the plaster wall next to my bed. What *was* that? I asked myself. I listened carefully for several minutes, while I rubbed my arm. "It was nothing," I decided. I was just about to go back to sleep when I heard the sound of glass breaking! I hopped out of bed and reached for the golf club!

24

Mrs. Marzipan's class studied space travel as their science topic for April and before long the children in the class were divided into two groups: those who believed that flying saucers existed and that beings from other planets had visited earth many times in the recent past; and those who thought that anybody who believed in flying saucers was nuts.

Ruth believed in flying saucers. Her next-door neighbor Andrew did not.

Every morning, as they walked to school, and every afternoon, as they walked home, they argued. Sometimes Ruth had company with her, people who took her side, and Andy found himself out-shouted and out-argued. Sometimes some of his supporters walked him home and Ruth found herself argued into silence.

"Where's the proof," Andy would say. "There's never been any proof that these flying saucers ever came here!"

"What about the photographs," Ruth would say. She meant that once in a while somebody who thought he or she saw a flying saucer took a snapshot of it, which was then published in a newspaper or a magazine.

"They're all blurry!" Andy would say. "You can't tell a thing from them."

"That's because of the radiation field from the flying saucers, it fogs up the film," Ruth would explain, "and they don't want people to know that they're visiting earth, anyway."

"Phooey," Andy would say. "What the heck would they want to visit this planet for, if they can travel all over the universe? What do we got that they'd have to come here for?"

"They want to see what we're doing with our atomic weapons," Ruth would say.

"Phooey," Andy would say, but nicely.

He and Ruth were good friends. Of course they argued the same points over and over again, but they enjoyed the arguments so much, they didn't mind.

A few days after the United States landed its Viking rocket on the surface of Mars, and photos were sent back to earth that seemed to show that Mars was a barren desert, Andy and Ruth sat in the candy store after school drinking milkshakes and talking about the Mars pictures.

"I guess there's no little green men up there, huh," Andy said. He slurped his milkshake.

"They haven't completed all the scientific tests," Ruth said, calmly. "There may be life in the soil of Mars."

"Phooey," said Andy. "If there were Martians up there, they would've zapped that rocket right away before it even got to the ground!"

"Oh, Andy," Ruth said, "if only you had a more open mind about the subject."

"My mind is open," Andy grinned. "But it's not as open as the minds of people who believe in little purple men from outer space. They have such open minds, they have holes in their heads!" He laughed.

Ruth laughed, too. They were good friends.

Andy liked to fish. His favorite lake was a few miles out in the country. Almost every Saturday he packed his gear and rode out to try his luck.

This Saturday he got up very early, got dressed and tip-toed past his parents' room, where they were still sleeping (he could hear his father snoring, although the bedroom was shut), and went downstairs and made himself some breakfast. Then he fixed some sandwiches, and cooked a hard-boiled egg for lunch.

Soon he was riding through the almost-deserted countryside. A few birds were twittering. The air was very still. The sun was barely up and dew sparkled on all the bushes and weeds by the side of the road. It was a little chilly and Andy shivered inside his jacket.

As he rode along he thought he heard a strange, low noise. At first it was so low he wondered if he heard it at all, but it gradually got louder and he knew he wasn't imagining it. Then he rounded a turn in the road and what he saw caused him to brake so hard he almost fell off his bike.

In the large empty field ahead of him was a huge metal object, rumbling softly like an old window fan. It hovered ten feet above the ground and the grass under it waved back and forth, slowly, although Andy could feel no wind. It was perfectly smooth, the color of pewter, and shaped like a huge soup dish turned upside down.

Andy climbed off his bike, but was so frightened he couldn't move very far. Fear locked his knees. As he watched and listened, the rumbling noises very, very slowly softened. When they stopped, a humming noise began. Then, a perfect circle appeared on the side of the object, and a hatch door slowly slid open . . .

25

Mr. Williamson always told us that he wasn't really a mean teacher, that he always tried to be fair to us. Well, maybe he did try to be fair, but a lot of times he was just plain mean. Like when it came to trips and gym. If you didn't behave well during the week, he didn't let you go to gym. If you really gave him trouble, he didn't take you along on trips. He was always giving little speeches about how everyone in the class was responsible for the whole class on a trip, and that if he couldn't trust *everyone*, he wasn't going to take *anyone*. That really wasn't too fair for the kids in the class who behaved themselves most of the time. They had to suffer for the stinkers.

Okay, I'm not an angel, that's for sure. Every year, my teacher tells my mother that I have potential, but I don't work up to my ability. Sure, I gave Mr. Williamson some trouble. Could I help it if the other children in the class distracted me all the time? I wasn't the only bad one, there were lots of bad boys and girls in our class, but Mr. Williamson seemed to single me out from everybody if there was noise at our table, for instance. Why me? And could I help it if I kept losing my pencils and notebook? Could I help it if I had to go to the bathroom all the time?

This April our class had planned a trip to the Museum of Natural History. I don't know how I managed to be taken along on that trip. Maybe Mr. Williamson had softened up a bit. Maybe my mother had sent him ten dollars in an envelope. I'll tell you one thing, though, not only did I get warned and lectured by Mr. Williamson the day before the trip, but Mr. Ashton, the principal, had a little discussion with me, too.

I didn't want to get left back, did I? I wanted to go on the rest of the great trips Mr. Williamson had planned, didn't I? I didn't want to upset my mother again, did I?

"Uh-huh!" I said.

"Okay!" Mr. Ashton then said. "This is it for you! Last warning! Here!" He handed me a cookie from the big glass jar he keeps on his desk, for when he gets hungry after lunch.

I looked him right in the eye. I said, "I'll try to behave tomorrow, Mr. Ashton."

"I believe you!" he said. "Now hurry back to your class and don't get lost in the building someplace again!"

Was I good on that trip! A couple of times Mr. Williamson came over to me and asked me if I felt all right. I didn't even talk to the other students. I stayed away from anyone who made *any* noise.

And what a great museum! Dinosaur skeletons and big stuffed whales and birds and Eskimos in long canoes and gorillas and totem poles! I didn't even have *time* to be bad. Once, Mrs. Freeman, my friend Howard's mother, who had come along on the trip with the class, told me to close my mouth before a fly flew in. I must have been staring at something with my mouth open.

After lunch we went to the auditorium and saw a film about Columbus discovering America, kind of boring. It was hot and stuffy in there, too. Mr. Williamson was sort of jittery. He kept saying over and over to Mrs. Freeman and to the other parent (I don't know whose father he was), "If this thing doesn't end pretty soon, we'll miss our bus!" He was really jittery. He kept taking his hanky out to wipe his forehead.

Finally, the film ended and the lights went on. Mr. Williamson said, "Okay, come on! Get in a line! Follow me! Take your partner's hand!" (We weren't little children, and we didn't hold hands, but he liked to say things like that.) "Let's go!" What a racket there was from all the classes in the auditorium! We sure left in a hurry. Mr. Williamson was really afraid that the bus driver would leave without us.

All of a sudden, I felt an urge.

"Mr. Williamson," I said, "I got to go to the bathroom!"

"When you get back to school! Come on! We'll miss the bus!"

"But I *got* to!" I insisted. "Emergency!"

"I said we'll miss the bus!" Boy, was he in a hurry.

Well, I had an emergency, and I knew I couldn't wait until we got back to school. I had to take care of myself. I thought to myself, "I'll just slip off the line and run outside after I'm done and meet them. I'll be so quick they won't even miss me. They'll never leave without me anyway."

So, as the class rushed down the corridors of the museum behind our teacher and his long legs, I slipped away. No one noticed me leave the line.

Where was the bathroom? I didn't even know.

I looked around. Next to a display case in which an Eskimo woman was fishing through a hole in the ice was a door, with a sign on it that said, "Employees Only." Maybe there's one in there, I thought. There were no guards around, so I opened the door carefully. There was no one inside. I walked a short distance, then through another door. Wherever I was, the place was deserted. "Hey," I said, "there it is!" An olive-green painted door was marked *Lavatory.* I pushed open the door, entered, and pulled it shut behind me. Then I heard two sounds: the click of the lock and a *clunk* as the old glass doorknob hit the floor. It broke into two pieces and the round part rolled under the sink.

"Uh-oh!" I said.

26

Every day after school, my friends and I would go to the playground and hang around for a while before we went home. Like most playgrounds, this one had an area with sandboxes and swings and seesaws for the little kids, basketball courts in another part for the older kids, and benches for mothers and old people. At one end was a softball field, not too big, but none of the boys in the group was strong enough to hit one over the fence yet, so it was big enough for them, when they got to use it.

Most of the time we all just watched the older guys play—the boys in our group watched the game, and the girls watched the players. These older guys, we all thought, must have been hooky players or school dropouts, because no matter how soon after three o'clock we got to the park, they were already there, playing softball, drinking soda and beer, cursing, yelling, sweating, cheering, smoking. They had a good time, all right. Sometimes, if we were lucky, they'd let us borrow the field to play a little while they rested. I guess they weren't there when it rained. I don't know, because neither were we.

Billy was the first in our group to start smoking, and I think the only reason he did it was to show one of the big kids that he, Billy, wasn't just a little punk. He wanted to show us, too.

One day we were leaning on the fence watching a softball game when one of the guys on the team that was batting passed by, puffing on a cigarette, and said to Billy, "Hey, Pee Wee, you want a drag?" He thought he was being funny, because Billy was about two feet shorter than he was. He meant it as a joke, but Billy took him seriously.

"Sure!" he answered. "Gimme that!" He took a few puffs, coughed, and handed the cigarette back. "Not bad," he managed to say. "What brand is that?" As if he knew one brand from the other!

He coughed for about fifteen minutes.

It wasn't long before several girls and boys in our bunch were pretending to act cool and grown-up as soon as we got to that playground. We'd stand by the basketball courts and watch the games and try not to choke to death as we smoked. None of us had much money, so we chipped in to buy a pack and split it up. We must have been a sight! Not one of us could really inhale smoke—we'd just take a little into our mouths and then let it out. Of course, we were careful to make sure that nobody we knew, or who knew our parents, was in that area of the park, because our parents had no idea that we were smoking. But, as I said, the courts were down at the end of the park, away from the benches.

As for me, I went along with the gang. I had a secret, though. I practiced at home.

I lived in a big home, and my room was at one end, three rooms away from my parents' bedroom. It was safe.

Late one night I sat by my open window and took a cigarette from my secret hiding place and lit it. I was trying to teach myself to blow smoke rings, but I wasn't having much success. I just couldn't get any smoke into my lungs without burning the back of my throat and coughing my head off. I had a towel on the window sill next to me to cough into, to muffle the sounds. My mother has excellent hearing, and she isn't the world's soundest sleeper.

Have you ever found that sometimes when you are thinking about something or other, or you're really tired, your mind drifts off and you don't think about what you are doing, you kind of do the motions automatically? Well, I was thinking about a movie I had just seen on television earlier in the evening, a western with Clint Eastwood in it. After I lit my cigarette I threw the burnt-out match into the trash can near my desk instead of out the window as I always do. It was just an automatic motion. I sat and blew smoke out the window and coughed into the towel when I had to. When the cigarette burned down I stubbed it out on the window ledge and tossed it away into the night. I was getting really sleepy. I yawned and said to myself, "Bedtime."

As I got up from my chair I turned around and noticed all the smoke in the room. It was coming from the wastepaper basket! I rushed over to the basket just as some orange tongues of flame leaped up and caught the bottom of the window curtain!

27

I had always kept my nose clean. You know what I mean. I had kept myself out of trouble, in school and out. I followed rules and regulations and did whatever I was supposed to do. That's the way my mom raised me. "Child," she always said to me, "the only way you will ever get someplace in this world is to be a good boy now and learn all you can and stay out of trouble. Once you get your share of the good things this world wants to offer you, then you can start to relax. School is very important. You have to work hard now and listen to your teachers and stay away from bad influences! You'll have lots of time to relax later. Remember, there's an old saying, 'Laugh now, cry later.' Well, I have my own. 'Apply yourself now, relax and enjoy later.'"

I *was* good, but you know, it's awfully hard to be good *all* the time. I couldn't keep away from the other boys and girls who misbehaved *all the time.* After all, some of them were in my class, and we all lived in the same neighborhood. I didn't join in when they did foolish things, but I did hang around with them sometimes.

Richard Wray was the leader of the troublemakers in my class. This bunch of girls and boys looked up to him because he seemed so brave and happy-go-lucky all the time. He didn't seem to care about what he did in school. He just laughed. He laughed in Mrs. Marzipan's face whenever she reprimanded him, and that made her even angrier. The other fools admired him for being such a big shot.

One day after lunch, Richard came into class late, sat down, and took six or seven small plastic cars and trucks out of his jeans pocket. He had just slicked them from Woolworth's, he said. His band of worshippers was impressed, so impressed that after school that afternoon a bunch of them, two boys and three girls, went on a "slicking expedition" (that's what they called the trip) and came back with their pockets bulging with small toys.

"It's simple!" they claimed the next morning, as they displayed their loot. Soon, they were slicking from the department store almost every day. They'd come back after lunch with little cars and animals and dolls, greeting cards, candy, pens, even things they didn't need, like thimbles. "It's easy," they boasted. "You just walk around and wait until there's no clerk near you, then you put the thing in your pocket and calmly walk out the door. And then run! It's easy!"

Now, as I said, I wasn't really in that gang, although I knew them all, and I sometimes played with them in the yard, but one day Felicia, Richard's girlfriend, said to me, "Hey, we're going slicking in Woolworth's after school. Want to come?"

"Me?" I said. "Not me! I don't want to be sent to jail!"

"Jail?" said Felicia. "Don't be a chicken. What are you, a chicken?"

Well, I didn't want them to think that I was a coward. I sure didn't want them to start calling me names. I thought for a little while, then said, "Okay. I'll go along. But just to watch. I'll watch how you do it. But I'm not going to steal anything."

"Yeah," said Felicia, smiling. "You'll see how easy it is!"

After school we met in the yard. Five or six of us walked to the store. We left our books behind a trash bin in the alley next to Woolworth's and went in. I felt real funny, and a little nervous. I stayed apart from the others and watched them.

I was amazed! They calmly walked around from counter to counter, keeping their eyes alert for clerks or manager, and every once in a while one of them took a little something from one of the displays and put it into his pocket—plastic soldiers, pencil sharpeners, even tins of aspirin! I couldn't believe my eyes!

I was standing about ten feet behind Richard when he suddenly said in a low voice without moving his lips, "I think we better get out of here! I think the manager just spotted me! Let's go!"

Richard headed for the door. The others noticed and

began to follow. So did I. I almost laughed—they looked so funny, walking as fast as they could, but not running! As soon as they got to the door, they *ran!* As Richard and I got to the front of the store he stopped for a moment.

"Here," he said to me, "hold this for me." He shoved a bunch of stuff into my hands, then took off.

I stood there, stupidly, staring at the things he had just given me. A voice yelled, "Hold it, you!" and somebody grabbed my arm!

28

Some people collect stamps and some people collect coins. Others collect bottle caps, baseball cards, books, or records. My dad collected old comic books, and what a collection he had!

He kept the comics in a metal case in his closet and took them out every so often to show to his friends or to company, or when he had an afternoon off and just felt like reading some. If he was in a good mood he took them out for my sister and me, if we asked him. We weren't allowed to touch any.

He had hundreds of comics in his collection, each in its own plastic bag. He had *Superman* and *Batman*, the *Jimmy Olsen* and *Lois Lane* comics that came out before I was born. He owned *Plastic Man, Human Torch, Justice League of America,* and all sorts of other very old things that he had since he was a kid. He especially liked Walt Disney comics and had a complete "run" as he called it, of

Uncle Scrooge, Walt Disney Comics and Stories, and *Donald Duck.* He liked *Little Lulu,* too. There were some comics he wouldn't let me or my sister see—the horror comics. These were especially valuable, he said. That was the reason he wouldn't even take them out of the plastic bags. Of course he owned a lot more recent things, like Marvel comics—he had ten copies of the first *Spider Man,* for instance, and he was always complaining that he hadn't had enough sense to buy a hundred of them when he could have paid a dime apiece at the newsstands. Comics used to be only ten cents each, he said. And they were thick! Not like the skinny ones you get for a quarter these days.

My dad bought a lot of comics in old bookstores and traded with other comic collectors. Sometimes my mother got annoyed at him because he spent so much money on them—I once heard him tell a friend he had paid over one hundred dollars for a few of the old *Superman* comics! But if my mother complained he'd say, "Comics are a good investment! Look at this *Human Torch!* I paid a dime for it in 1946! Now it's worth over three hundred dollars! What if I had put that dime in the bank? How much would I have now?" He had figured it out. The dime would be worth about seventy-one cents if he had left it in the bank.

My dad guarded his collection carefully, so carefully, in fact, that he almost never let anyone take a comic out of its plastic bag to get a good look at it. If he did allow somebody to handle one, he watched him like a hawk. Once he came home a little early from work and found me reading some old Archie comics (he had dozens of them) which were scattered all over the living room floor. Did he blow his top! I got punished. I was very young then, but I learned my lesson. From then on, whenever I felt like reading some of the comics in my dad's collection, I made sure whatever I read was back in its place well before he got home.

One day in school I overheard two of my classmates, Joe and Helen, talking about comic books. They were talking about recent things, *The Hulk, The Fantastic Four,* things like that, which anybody with a quarter could get at the newsstand. I butted in.

"Do you know what my dad has?" I said. "He's got old, valuable comics! He's got *Uncle Scrooge Number One!* He's even got comics from World War II, over thirty years ago!" I was showing off a little, I guess. I didn't like Joe or Helen very much anyway, because *they* were always bragging about something.

They didn't believe a word I said.

"It's true!" I insisted. "He's got lots of old comics in his collection!"

"Yeah, sure," said Helen. She laughed.

Because my feelings were hurt, I foolishly said, "I'll bring some in tomorrow and show you!"

"I'll believe it when I see it!" said Joe. He looked at Helen and they laughed.

My father left for work very early in the morning. I ate my breakfast, and while my mother was feeding my sister, I snuck up to my parents' room, went to my father's closet, and took out the metal box. I planned to take a few comics into school and then bring them back home at three o'clock and put them away again. My dad would never notice they had been gone for a few hours.

Since the comics were carefully arranged I had no trouble finding *Uncle Scrooge Number One,* or any of the *Justice League of America* comics from World War II. I put these into a big yellow envelope, put the box back into the closet, went downstairs, and left for school.

As soon as I got to school, Joe came over to my table and said, "So where are they? Where are all those great old comics you said you were gonna bring in?"

"Right here," I said. Mrs. Anderson was busy in the front of the room, I observed, so I took the comics from my desk and put them on the table.

"Don't touch any of them, just look at them. Hey, don't touch . . ."

Some other kids noticed what I had taken out and crowded around my desk. Some were grabbing.

"Don't touch, hey!" I said, over and over. I was soon in the middle of a big commotion.

Suddenly they all scattered back to their chairs. Mrs. Anderson was looming over me, and frowning.

"What is this nonsense?" she yelled. "Why aren't you working? Put them away!"

I put all the comics in a neat stack. Then, Mrs. Anderson grabbed them from me, stalked over to her closet, and locked them up!

"Take out your math books!" she said, sourly, to the silent class.

"Those are my father's!" I said. "They're from his collection! That's *Uncle Scrooge Number One!*"

"Well!" said Mrs. Anderson, very much annoyed. "Bring a note from your father and I'll give them back. I said all math books out!"

29

We had the quietest, neatest section in the room until Mrs. Marzipan moved that new kid, Peter, over here. He was transferred from Mrs. Glim's class into ours because he couldn't get along with the kids in there—that's what the story was. And she had to move him over here! He spoiled everything.

He was afraid of Mrs. Marzipan for the first few days and was pretty quiet, but he sure caused trouble in his sneaky, secret way. For instance, he loved to rip up paper into little snowflakes and throw them on the floor. He spent hours doing it, but Mrs. Marzipan never noticed. Naturally it got scattered under our seats and tables and made our whole area messy. Our tables used to be nice and straight until he got here. Peter moved around so much he knocked every table out of line. We had to fix them fifty times a day. When we weren't looking, he'd take colored Magic Markers or crayons and make streak marks on our tabletops. He'd push our books off the table and onto the floor with a ruler, while he pretended to look in another direction. He was really a pest.

I repeat, he didn't do anything *noisy* for the first couple of days. He'd kick us under the table, or kick our chair legs as we tried to work. That didn't make any noise, but it was very annoying. He wrote little notes and stuck them in other people's books: *Gerald thinks you are pretty, signed George,* or *Michael said you are a punk, signed Jeff.* He just seemed to like to annoy people. When our class lined up to go to another place in the building or down to lunch, as he stood by the bulletin board he'd scribble all over the excellent work Mrs. Marzipan had hung up. As for *his* work, he didn't do much. Usually, after a little prodding from Mrs. Marzipan, he *seemed* to begin, but he never got much beyond writing the heading and the "Aim," and maybe one or two sentences. Then he'd look around at the rest of us working and find some way to bother us.

After a week or so he got bolder, and began to devote a lot of time to getting *me* steamed up.

I'm very fussy, you see. I've always been a good student and I've always listened and I always try to do perfect work. My mother says the only perfect beings are angels, but I still try to be perfect. I'm very particular about everything, down to the last period, margins, spaces, everything. It didn't take Peter long to notice these things about me. He began to annoy me. He'd say, "How's your commas, Henrietta?" (Henrietta isn't even my name, it's Lois!) "Don't forget those margins! Capital D over there!" Do you know how mad you can get when you hear things like that all day? I tried to ignore Peter, but he had such a stupid grin on his face that I felt like throwing my math book at it. The angrier I got, the more mistakes I made, even ones I would never make, like putting commas in the wrong places. Oh, I was really bothered! Plus, of course, he had not abandoned his old tricks: he'd say, "Hey, Henrietta, how do you like this rhythm?" and tap his pencil, and *grin* at me.

Mrs. Marzipan didn't do anything about it. She had the regular class problems to worry about. Ronald and Francis and Felix kept her pretty busy. Since what Peter did was mostly quiet and local (he didn't bother the children at the other tables much) she hardly ever paid attention to what he did.

One afternoon we were working on social studies. Mrs. Marzipan was across the hall in Mr. Ashton's room, asking him a question about a film strip. We all had blank maps of the eastern half of the United States and, with the help of our social studies books, we were filling in the products and industries and rivers and major cities of all the different states. I like map work. I'm even fussier about my map work than I am about most of my other subjects. That's pretty fussy!

I had been working very carefully with a felt-tipped pen, and I was almost done. As usual, Peter was doing nothing. He didn't even have a map in front of him. He had made an airplane out of it and thrown it somewhere. He was leaning back in his chair, watching the rest of us work. Suddenly, he lost his balance—he fell backwards, and he and his chair crashed to the floor! I was so startled, my pen made a long, green streak across my map from Ohio to Massachusetts.

I was so mad and angry I lost my temper! I stood over Peter and, as soon as he got to his feet, grinning, I shoved him as hard as I could. He tripped over his chair, fell down again, and began to cry.

"Lois! What did you just do!" shouted Mrs. Marzipan from the doorway. She had just come in. "You hurt him! Peter, are you all right?"

30

A large, wooded island lay way out in the middle of the lake. People called it simply "the island"; it had no regular name. Nobody knew who owned it. People said that years and years ago an old couple had lived in a cabin on the island and buried a lot of money somewhere in the woods. Once in a while the old man would row in and come into town to buy some supplies, matches or candles or toothpaste (no one knew why the man needed toothpaste, he didn't have any teeth). He also bought ammunition. There was game on the island: deer and all sorts of smaller animals like rabbits, squirrels, raccoons, probably skunks. Many, many years ago, folks said, there had been bears and wolves out there too. It was a pretty big island. As far as anyone knew, nobody lived there anymore.

One summer morning, Ruth and Andy and Penny and Joel biked to the lake shore for a picnic lunch. After they ate their chicken sandwiches, they built a little fire and roasted some marshmallows. Then they carefully extinguished the fire and sat with their backs against the trees and stared out over the shining lake to the island. The sun was high in the sky, and it was hot. Andy threw pebbles into the water. They made little *glink!* sounds as they sunk.

"There's that island," said Ruth.

"Yeah," said Andy. "The Island."

"Did your dad every tell you the story about the funny old people who used to live there years ago?" Penny asked.

All the children knew the story, but wanted to hear it again. It was the kind of story that got better each time you heard it, because people liked to add new things to it each time it was told.

"Let's hear it!" Joel said.

So Penny told the story and finished by saying, "And to this day nobody knows what happened to the old couple! Some people say their ghosts are still there, in a cabin in the middle of the woods, and they only come out at night to guard their treasure!"

The children smiled and gazed out over the water at the island. There was a haze on the lake now. The vegetation on the island was the exact color of a glob of cooked spinach.

"I wonder what it's really like out there," said Ruth.

"There's only one way to find out!" said Joel. "And that's to go there!" He stood up. "And I know just the way to do it! Follow me!"

Earlier, Joel had noticed a row boat hidden in a little cove, so they biked back about a quarter of a mile to that spot. The boat was tied to a tree. There were two oars.

"Do you think we should?" asked Penny.

"Well, we're not stealing the boat," said Andy, "only borrowing it! We'll bring it back. Come on!"

So they camouflaged their bikes under some bushes and set forth. They took turns rowing. The island was pretty far out, and the sun was very strong, but they were all excited about the adventure. No one in their little group had ever been to the island before.

About half way to the island a breeze picked up and the ride became more pleasant.

After much strenuous rowing, they were offshore. Now they looked for a good place to land. Along most of the shore, thick, dark woods grew right down to the water, while other parts were marshy and shallow. Tall cattails waved in the breeze. Sunning turtles on half-sunken logs dropped off as soon as they got too close, and swam away. Many red-winged black birds, with their red and yellow wing patches, flew about.

They soon found a sandy spot to land, and Joel, who was rowing, eased the boat in as well as he could. Then they all hopped out and stretched their arms and legs. Before them was a grass-covered slope. Beyond that, the tall woods began. It was now past mid-day and a heavy silence hung over the island. The only sounds were the *clop! clop!* of the water on the bottom of the row boat, and a slight tinkling sound the shallow waves made as they died in the debris on the shore. Even the crows seemed to be asleep.

They stood and stared for many minutes at the woods. The kids thought about all the stories they had heard about this famous and mysterious place—about wild animals, the strange old couple, ghosts, treasure.

It was Andy who first broke out of the trance. It occurred to him that a certain sound was missing. He thought for a few moments, then realized what it was: he could no longer hear the *clop!* of the waves on the bottom of the boat.

He turned around.

"Hey!" he yelled, "the boat's gone!" He splashed into the shallow water waving his arms. "It's gone!"

The others turned to look. The boat, minus its oars which still lay on the sand, was already hundreds of feet out and drifting rapidly away.

"Oh, no!" cried Penny.

31

We moved again last June, to an apartment on the fifth floor of an old building. I guess it was big enough for me and my noisy baby sister and my mother; at least, it was bigger than the place we had lived in before it, and much bigger than the place before that. But I didn't like the place. Of course, it's hard to tell what your new apartment is really like with all the clothes and furniture and stuff still in cartons all over the place and the windows dirty (one of them was broken and it took a long time to get the super to come up and fix it), but I just didn't like the place.

As for my new street, there seemed to be hundreds of people sitting all over the stoops, leaning on cars, standing in doorways, and some even lying on the sidewalks. They never seemed to do anything except drink soda and beer and then throw the empty cans and bottles into the gutter or into the hallways or the alley. They always made a lot of noise, so much that you could hear the hollering and the fighting and the laughing and the radios and the little portable phonographs all the way up to our floor—even with the windows closed—late into the night. Since the weather was getting hot we couldn't keep the windows shut, or we would have roasted. So I couldn't sleep too well and neither could my sister or my mother. My sister bawled all the time and my mother was even more short-tempered with me than she usually was. It seemed like I was always under her feet, getting in the way. She kept yelling at me to get out of the house, but I didn't. I just stayed upstairs. I managed to stay away from her while all the stuff lay around in a big mess. It hid me a little.

I was afraid to go out of the house. From my window I could see up and down the street, and I was afraid. There seemed to be two or three bunches of girls and boys who just ran up and down the block all day making noise and causing trouble. Sometimes they carried sticks. They bothered the older people on the stoops and they threw garbage around and really messed the street up. They tipped over garbage cans and climbed all over parked cars. Once they set fire to a pile of trash. I was scared of those kids.

So, I just moped around the house and tried to keep out of my mother's way. When she wasn't in the front room I would look out the window. You could see pretty far from the window. On clear days, I could see the river and the bridges and the ships, over the tops of the smaller buildings across the street.

Of course, once in a while I had to go out of the house. I took the garbage down for my mom, but I always checked through the window first to make sure none of those wild kids were around. Then I hurried down with the trash and dumped it outside in the can and scooted back up. I never stayed outside.

One morning my mom yelled at me, "I want you out of here! Get some fresh air! Go play in the street!" She was tired, and my sister was crying again in the other room. I had to leave. My mom watched me put on my sneakers, then watched me let myself out the front door.

Carefully I went down one flight and then stuck my head out the hallway window on the fourth floor to see what was going on in the street. It was only about nine-thirty, very early in the morning, and things were pretty quiet. There weren't many people hanging around yet. Best of all, I didn't see any of those wild kids. Just trash cans and broken glass that glittered like diamonds and an old dog sniffing about.

On the first floor I did the same thing I did on the fourth: I carefully looked around, before I took my body out into the open. Things looked safe. I said to myself, "Nobody around here this early."

I started to bounce my ball against the stoop steps, playing points. Do you know that game? You try to hit the point of the step just right so the ball flies back to you without bouncing, and you get a point. I had just gotten my seventh point when I heard a voice holler from across the street behind me, "Hey! Hey!" Then, "Hey, you!" I turned around—and froze. Coming down the front steps of the tenement right across the street was a bunch of kids—girls and boys, about five or six of them. They crossed the street. One of them was carrying a stick.

32

Ruth loved the play *Peter Pan*, and every time the production with Mary Martin as Peter was shown on TV, she watched it. She had seen the Walt Disney movie and had read the original play and book by J.M. Barrie lots of times. So when Mrs. Strang, the teacher in charge of the annual school play, announced that this year's PTA fund-raising production would be *Peter Pan*, she just knew she had to try out for it! She had to get one of the big parts!

She had always been a ham, her mother told her; she started to act when she was in her playpen. She couldn't remember that far back, but she did know that she had always liked to dress up in costumes whenever she got the chance, and act. She always tried to get good parts in class plays. In the first grade she played a broken window in a play about safety. She played a drunken Hessian soldier once—you know about that party on New Year's Eve, when Washington crossed the frozen Delaware to surprise the celebrating English and the Hessians, during the Revolutionary War? And last year, she played Mrs. Spooky in the class Halloween play. She loved to act.

The tryouts were held in the auditorium, of course. Lots of kids were milling around, but Ruth wasn't worried.

She was not at all shy about getting up on stage and singing and speaking. First, Mrs. Strang asked each of the hopefuls to sing something. Ruth sang "You're a Grand Old Flag" in her best voice. She wasn't the greatest singer, but she projected, she thought—that meant she could be heard clearly about five miles away. Next, everyone had to read out of the script while Mrs. Strang sat all the way in the back of the auditorium.

Ruth had a good speaking voice. She read Wendy's father's famous speech about how he can't get his necktie tied around his neck, just around the bedpost. Wendy's father is really a grouchy guy. "One hundred times have I tied it around the bedpost, oh, yes, but around my neck, no! Begs to be excused!" It was fun. She knew she was good, too. Some kids clapped when she was done.

The next day, after lunch, she was standing next to Mrs. Marzipan's desk, waiting to ask a question about one of the math problems the class was working on, when a messenger from Mrs. Strang's class came into the room. He had a note for Mrs. Marzipan. The teacher put on her glasses and then read it. Her face got all scrunched up the way it did when she couldn't make out the handwriting.

"Oh," she said, pleasantly. She looked at Ruth. "Mrs. Strang wants you down in the auditorium at two o'clock. Something about the play."

Wow! Ruth felt so good, she clapped her hands! Maybe she'd get to play Wendy or Tinkerbell or Peter! Peter was always played by a girl. Ruth was really excited!

As it turned out, she did not get one of the big roles. She really didn't get *any* role. Mrs. Strang made her the understudy for Peter. You know what an understudy is? An understudy is an actor who learns the lines of a big part in case something happens to one of the stars and he or she can't go on. Then the understudy takes over.

Phooey! Ruth had to learn Peter's part and probably wouldn't even get to go on stage. She was terribly disappointed. She thought, how could Mrs. Strang have done such a thing to me, a great, potentially famous, actress like me?

When she got home that afternoon, her mother took one look at her and said, "What's the matter?"

Ruth told her.

"Well," Ruth's mother said, "I don't want to sound like I'm preaching, but it says in the Bible, 'Pride cometh before the fall,' and the Bible doesn't mean the autumn."

Ruth learned Peter's part. She didn't practice her lines in front of a mirror, like she usually did. She just learned the words. She didn't practice making any good Peter faces, or practice flying, or anything. She went to most of the rehearsals in the auditorium, but she hardly ever got to do anything except watch. One day Leona Harris, who had the role of Peter, was home with a cold, and Ruth was asked to read the part. But that was when everyone was still reading from scripts, and even though she knew she could have put on a good show for Mrs. Strang and everyone else, she didn't.

As the weeks went by and all the details fell into place, the scenery hung, and the costumes made, Ruth grew sadder and sadder. She sat in the first or second row of the auditorium, usually in the middle of the chorus, and sang along, but every time Leona came out on stage in her terrific green costume, topped by a green pixie hat with a feather, and carrying a little sword, Ruth felt terrible. She thought, I'm a better actress than she is! I can twirl around more gracefully than she can! She can't even get her plastic sword in and out of the scabbard without looking clumsy!

The last dress rehearsal took place on a Thursday afternoon. The big show was to be held that night at eight. The parents' association had been selling tickets for two weeks, and the show was a sellout! Ruth had to admit that the last dress rehearsal was great. Mrs. Strang and the children and Mrs. Weinglass and Mr. Murphy, who was in charge of the dancing and singing, had put together a terrific show.

But Ruth didn't even intend to go. What was she going to do, stand in the wings while Leona got all the glory? Not her! There was a good science fiction movie on TV and Ruth intended to watch it.

Ruth was in front of the TV set at seven-thirty that evening when the phone rang. Her mother answered it.

"It's for you!" she called. "It's Mrs. Strang and she sounds excited! She wants to know where you are!"

33

"Where was the subway, anyway?" I wondered as I stood on the platform. I was on my way home from school and I had been standing there for at least fifteen minutes. Of course, I was used used to waiting for late subway trains, but that didn't make the wait any less annoying.

I looked around the station for perhaps the fiftieth time—at the messy, scrawled-up walls, at the garbage on the tracks, the dirty ceilings with their dusty light bulbs. I thought: *The longer it takes the train to come, the more crowded it will be! More people will be getting into the same car as me!*

The station was already crowded with dozens of people and, as I looked at some of them, I got the creeps! All around me were sinister-looking teenagers wearing funny hats at crazy angles, old, unshaven men drinking beer or something else from bottles in little paper bags (it's illegal to drink intoxicating beverages in the subway, but that law never stopped anyone), old ladies with fat red legs and no teeth who dragged enormous stuffed shopping bags, young women cracking gum, and weary business men in wrinkled suits, with their ties loosened. A pretty average group of subway riders. *Where was that train?*

I had to get home. I had two tests the next day, and I hadn't even opened a book to study for either of them. Plus, my mother got all nervous and bothered if I didn't get home at my normal time. She still treated me as if I were eight years old. She had turned into a nervous wreck after my father went away. I was all she had left, she'd say. I tried to understand her concern about me, but it was tough, sometimes, to put up with it.

I looked around again and jingled the change in my coat pocket. I had a grand total of thirty-five cents, very little indeed. I had a few bucks at home. I just didn't like to carry much money, because I spent it if I did. I always tried to calculate in advance how much I'd need for the day, and carry that amount. As people say, you can't spend it if you don't have it with you.

Meanwhile, a short, bald man in a gray jacket, who had been standing near me for about five minutes, peered down the dark tunnel and said, half to me, half to himself, "This is for the birds. Every day it's like this. For the birds."

"Yeah," I said. I had to say something back. I don't like to talk to strangers. Riding in a crowded subway car for long periods of time makes me uneasy, too. It's hot and stuffy and smelly in those old cars, and people are always poking into you and jostling you. The noise can be absolutely deafening. Sometimes I have to hold my hands over my ears.

At last, I heard a distant rumbling sound and a few seconds later, with tremendous noise and vibrations, the train pulled into the station. A few people got off and many more, including me, got on.

There were no seats, of course. I stood between an overweight man with slicked-back grey hair who chewed gum and blew bubbles and a short, stout lady whose packages kept poking into the side of my chest every time the train swayed. The swaying of a subway car has a hypnotic effect on me. It dulls my mind and I half-dream, half-think about all sorts of things as I ride. This protects me, because if I keep my mind and eyes and nose and ears open to what is really happening around me, practically on top of me, I have no insulation. So, there I was, holding onto a handle attached to the ceiling, swaying, half-awake, half-dreaming, protected.

Several minutes later, after a few stops, the train entered a long tunnel. The train rode for about two minutes and gradually slowed down, then stopped. This commonly happens when a signal light in the tunnel is red. It usually goes green in a minute or two, but the train sat and didn't move.

Passengers grumbled, then began to complain to one another about the poor service. "Happens all the time." "A crying shame, in the *greatest city in the world!* Ha!" "No consideration for the public." "A cattle car, that's what this is." "Why don't they let us know what's holdin' us up?"

The subway train sat. The car got warmer and warmer. I noticed that the lights in the car were flickering. Then they grew dim. Up and down the whole train, the lights went out.

"Oh, my God," somebody cried, "a power failure!"

34

My father and I really went through some tough times after my mom died. We never seemed to have enough money. My dad got sick a lot, and he missed work. His boss told him that if he stayed out sick too often, he'd have to fire him, so he went to work even when he didn't feel too well. Then, when he got home, he'd just lie on his bed and stare at the ceiling. Sometimes, he'd cry to himself. I didn't know what to do. I tried to get after-school jobs to earn some money to help out in the house, but all the storekeepers in the neighborhood said I was too young and wouldn't hire me. Sometimes they gave me little jobs to do for fifty cents, like sweeping the floor, but a few cents didn't really help.

Then, we had to move to a less expensive apartment in a whole new, strange neighborhood, where neither my father nor I knew anybody, and I found myself in a new school, in a new class.

It didn't take me long to get into trouble. Not really serious trouble, but trouble serious enough to make my father sad every time he got another letter from my new teacher, Mrs. Elliot. You see, we couldn't afford a telephone now, so the only way Mrs. Elliot could get in touch with my father was to send him notes in the mail. Every time my father read one of those notes, he moaned softly to himself. Then he'd go into his room to lie down. I felt so terrible each time this happened that I promised my father I'd behave. It tore me up to see what I was doing to him.

But I just couldn't help myself. There were some know-it-all kids in my new class who took me under their wings like I was one of the family. I don't really know why, but almost as soon as I started to hang around with them after school, I forgot most of the things my father and my teachers had taught me about behavior, respect, and manners. I can't explain it. I changed. I had never stolen from the Five and Ten before I met them. I had never talked back to a teacher. I had always done my schoolwork as well as I could. I had always come home for supper on time. I had hardly ever used curse words, although of course, they used to slip out once in a while.

One Friday afternoon there I was again, sitting next to another troublemaker on a bench in the assistant principal's office, feeling miserable. I worried about how my father would react to the letter Mrs. Elliot was going to write that evening. We had been sent out of the room because we had scribbled up each other's notebooks, right in the middle of a math lesson. I don't know why I did it, except that when somebody scribbles in my book, I scribble right back. *Another letter home,* I thought to myself. I knew my father would be very unhappy when he saw it.

I must have said those words out loud, because my companion, who was not very upset, said, "Why don't you do what I do?"

"What's that?" I said.

"Intercept the mail!" was the answer. "Rip up the

letter before your father sees it. Then he won't know nothing!"

"Yeah, great," I said, sourly. "I don't even have a key to the mailbox."

"Have one made for fifty cents! Then you can check the mail when you get home from school, take the letter out, and when your pa takes the mail out of the box later when he gets home from work, he won't know nothing!"

As I sat on the bench, I thought about this idea. The more I thought about it, the better it seemed. Finally, I decided to do it. It really wouldn't do me any good, but at least it would keep my father from getting upset again.

Saturday afternoon, while my dad took a nap, I took his keys from the kitchen table and went to the hardware store to have a copy made of our mailbox key. I put his keys back in the same spot. Mrs. Elliot's letter wouldn't arrive until Monday or Tuesday, so I knew I'd be able to get to it before my father saw it.

As soon as I got home from school on Monday, I looked in the mailbox. There was some stuff in it, mostly bills, I supposed, but no letter. Mrs. Elliot always used school stationery, so P.S. 184 and the school address were always in the upper-left corner of the envelope.

All during the day Tuesday I was on pins and needles. I ran home at three o'clock. When I got to the lobby, out of breath, I bent down and peered into our mailbox. It was jammed, but sure enough, pressed right up against the little window, I could see the school address! I had to get that envelope out! I reached into my pocket for the key.

There was no key in my pocket. There was nothing in my pocket except a big hole!

Before I could think about what to do next, I heard a voice. I looked up.

It was my father. "Is that you?" he said.

He had just come into the lobby and he didn't look too good.

"Dad, what's the matter?!" I cried. I was frightened. "Why are you home so early?"

He didn't answer me. He put his arms around me, and hugged me to him and I thought he was going to cry.

35

When I was young, I lived with my Aunt Sarah, and she treated me as if I were her own child. She not only fed me and bought me clothes, she also helped me with my homework when I had problems with it. She went to school on Open School Days to talk with my teachers. She also punished me when I did something wrong or misbehaved, which happened every once in a while. Yes, she treated me as if she were my real mother. I loved her.

One year early in December I lay on the bed in my room, staring at the ceiling. I was upset. It was the time of year when everybody begins to think about Christmas presents, those they hope to receive and those they hope to give. I wasn't thinking about what I wanted. I was thinking about what I wanted to get for my Aunt Sarah.

I had very little money then. My aunt gave me fifty cents a week allowance, part of which I managed to save. Aunt Sarah didn't have very much money herself. She worked in a bakery and sold cookies and cakes and did not earn a big salary, but she still gave me fifty cents a week. She also received a little money each month from the government, because her husband had been killed during the Second World War, while in the navy.

During the past three months I had saved about two dollars. I knew exactly what I wanted to get for my aunt, if only I had had more money. I passed a thrift shop every afternoon on my way home from school and in the front window was a beautiful china pitcher and saucer, decorated with tiny blue and yellow flowers. I knew my aunt would love it. She owned a very few pieces of china that her husband had sent her from overseas before he was killed, but she didn't own a pitcher and saucer. I paused on my way home every afternoon to look in the store window. One day, I had finally gone into the store to find out how much money the two pieces of china cost. The owner of the shop, a little old man with white hair who puffed on an old, dark wooden pipe, had lifted the china carefully from the window and blown some dust from it. He had turned the pitcher over to show me what was written, baked in, on the bottom: *Bone China. Made in England.* "These are two nice pieces," the old man had said, "from England. I can let you have them both for five dollars." He had looked at me and then puffed on his pipe. My heart sank. I thanked him and left the store. Then as I lay on my bed, I thought and thought: *Where was I going to get three more dollars?*

I trudged slowly home from school. Christmas was coming closer and closer and I still didn't know how I was going to get the present for my Aunt Sarah. I stopped, as I did every day, in front of the store window to admire the china. It gleamed beautifully among the other wonderful and not so wonderful things on display: old lamps, books, small bronze statues, an old cash register, some candlesticks, an old doll. I sighed, and walked on.

I went into Mr. Walters's little grocery store to pick

up half a pound of ham and a can of soup for supper. Mr. Walters was very busy. He seemed to be waiting on four customers at the same time, but he still noticed me and said, "Hello, there! Still looking down in the mouth, I see!"

"Hello, Mr. Walters," I said. I liked Mr. Walters's grocery. It wasn't lit up like the A & P, but it was always nice and cool, even in the summer. It smelled of sour pickles, because there was a big, uncovered barrel of them standing near the front counter. There was sawdust on the floor and all sorts of cheeses and hams and sausages hung from the ceiling. What I liked most, though, was that Mr. Walters knew all his customers and said hello to them all. He was friendly. He had had his store in the neighborhood for over thirty years. I hated to go into supermarkets. The clerks and cashiers were always in a hurry. They just wanted to get you out of the store so they could wait on the next customer.

"Busy today," remarked Mr. Walters when I came back to the counter with a package of ham and a can of soup. "How's your aunt?"

"Fine," I said. I gave Mr. Walters a five dollar bill.

"Still looking down in the dumps, 'eh? Still can't get that pitcher, 'eh?"

I shook my head. I had told Mr. Walters all about it the week before.

"Well," said the grocer, "you're a good child and she'll like whatever you get her. Here's your change!"

I took the change and stuffed it in my pocket. "So long, Mr. Walters," I said to him.

"So long now. Sorry I can't talk today, got business." A woman in a long dark coat had dumped some cans of sardines on the counter and the grocer began to ring them up.

I walked slowly home, carrying my schoolbooks in

one hand and the purchases in the other. I had put my change into my pocket without counting it, because Mr. Walters was not only my friend, but the most honest man in the world. But the bills were all bunched up. I stopped, put my things down on a car, and took the money out of my pocket. As I straightened out the bills and folded them neatly my eyes opened wide. I counted the money three times. Mr. Walters had given me three dollars too much change.

36

My father sold his cleaning store last year and my whole family, my parents and me and my two little brothers, moved. My dad was supposed to open a card and gift shop out in a new suburban shopping center. But bad luck struck: the landlord rented to someone else, my dad couldn't open the store, and there just weren't any other good empty stores in the area. He looked in other places, but he couldn't find anything.

So there we were, in a strange, new neighborhood, with no business. At first, my father was really angry at the landlord. He stormed around the house swearing at him. Then, he quieted down and was sad. He just moped around the house. After a while he didn't even go out, and often sat around in his pajamas until after lunchtime. I'd come home from my new school, which I didn't like very much because the children were all strangers, to find my dad still in his pajamas, unshaven, smoking one cigarette after another. No money was coming into the house. Of course, we still had the money my dad had intended to use to open his new store, but that wasn't going to last forever.

At first, my mom was patient with my dad, because she knew how he felt, but after a month or more, because he just sat around, disgusted with himself, and wasn't even trying anymore to find a place to open a new business, she began to crab at him. He didn't want to work for anyone else. That was out of the question. He wanted to be his own boss. I heard him say those words a million times.

I understood how she felt, too. She was worried, not only about my father, but about the whole family. How were we going to eat if the savings ran out? How would we pay the bills? At first she tried prodding him, gently, and when that had no effect on my dad, she lost her patience. Most of the time he didn't even answer her. He'd get up and walk into another room and turn on the TV.

Then things really went bad.

My brothers and I didn't know what to do. My youngest brother, Anthony, was scared. He would ask me, "Why do they always fight?" and try not to cry. My other brother, Tom, who's very shy and quiet, tried to ignore what was going on in the house, but he couldn't. It was impossible to ignore what was happening.

The more quiet and subdued my father became, the more annoyed my mother became. She found fault with everything he did. She slammed his food down in front of him at the dinner table. She snatched the plate from him when he was finished. When the family ate together she often said things like, "Eat up, kids, eat everything! I don't know how long we'll be eating full meals in this house!" Then she'd glare at dad. He usually kept on chewing and said nothing. That made her even madder.

My brothers and I didn't understand what was going on. We got really frightened. After a couple of weeks of this, our home was like a crazy house. I saw the anger and fear in my mother's eyes and in the way she pinched up her mouth, and my dad sank deeper and deeper into himself, and didn't talk much anymore. He must have felt miserable, but he never complained that he did.

Things got worse and worse. My mother got dark circles under her eyes from worrying and she, too, began to smoke a lot of cigarettes. My two little brothers began to fall behind in their schoolwork. "He's not keeping his mind on his schoolwork," their teachers said to my mother when she went in to school to speak to them. As for me, I tried not to let what was happening at home affect *my* schoolwork, but it was hard. I couldn't concentrate on my work. I did what I had to do, but my mind wasn't in it. Sometimes I even hated school, and the unfriendly kids stayed far away from me, probably because they read the fear and worry on my face.

One night my brothers and I were wakened by shouts coming from our parents' bedroom. We were used to my mother's aggravated speech, but we had rarely heard her raise her voice. We stood in the doorway of our room, listening, frightened. Anthony held tight to the leg of my pajamas. Suddenly we heard a *thump*, and then a *crash!* The door to my parents' room opened and my father came out. He was dressed. He walked slowly right past us, took his coat from the hall closet, unlocked the front door, and went out.

37

James Baxter grew up in the whaling town of New Bedford, Massachusetts. In those days, in the 1830s, New Bedford was a bustling town, not sort of reserved like it is today. People don't use whale oil anymore like they did then. Why, a keg of whale oil was once worth a small fortune! And ambergris—that was what they called the solid piece of musky-smelling lumpy material that was sometimes found in a sperm whale's intestines—why, that was worth a king's ransom! Perfumes were made from that stuff! So people were willing to take off to sea to hunt whales, and bankers were willing to finance the journeys. It cost a lot of money to outfit a whale ship. A trip might take two to three years. A whale hunting expedition was mighty dangerous, too. A lot of good, brave men and a lot of fine ships never returned to New Bedford.

New Bedford was full of old sailors, veterans of many a whaling journey, who sat around on old kegs down by the docks and told tales to anybody who would listen. They told tales of whales so huge they were able to smash whaling boats with their fins; of South Pacific islands, where the natives liked nothing better than to have a sailor or two for Sunday dinner; of strange, calm stretches of sea in which ships drifted for weeks before a breath of wind stirred the sails. James and his friends listened time after time to these grey, weathered old men and stared at the tattoos on their skinny arms and at the necklaces of strange shells they wore around their necks.

Ever since James could recall, he had wanted to ship out and hunt whales. His parents knew this, but they insisted that he get some schooling first. He somehow managed to sit through seven boring years of school. His mind was not in the classroom much. It was out at sea, in a whale boat!

When James was twelve, he was old enough to be signed onto a vessel. Boys started work quite young in those days. His father signed him on as ship's boy on a whaling ship called the *Bully Boy*. The captain's name was Mr. Hardy. He had a face weathered by many a tropical sun and down his left arm, a long, jagged scar. Thirty-some years ago, he said, a harpoon pulled out of a whale's back had flown through the air and struck him. He had been around the world five times! When the captain told James's mother that they'd probably be gone for two or three years, she wiped tears from her eyes. But James's father didn't display any emotion. He said, "He will be a man when he comes back."

They set out from New Bedford in late April, 1837, and headed for the open sea. The *Bully Boy* was a stout ship and manned by a seasoned crew. James was treated terribly. The men made fun of his youth and lack of sea experience. But he learned quickly. He learned to repair ropes, sharpen harpoons, climb the masts, and walk the tilting decks. He soon learned to predict the weather by studying the clouds and the color of the sea. Within a few weeks he was a competent young sailor.

They didn't expect to reach the whale hunting grounds until the beginning of July, and a lot had to be done before they got there. All the long boats had to be checked out and supplied with tarred rope, sharpened harpoons, and knives. The ropes had to be carefully coiled so that when a harpooned whale took off, the rope uncoiled smoothly from the boat. If a rope caught a sailor's leg, it could drag him out of the boat. And each boat had to have extra sets of oars. Oars were always falling or getting knocked out of the long boats.

One morning James was helping an old sailor, Sam, in one of the long boats and was annoying him with his questions. Although he had heard descriptions of whale hunts from the old sailors on the docks, he still wanted to know from him, Sam, what it was like to go out after the huge animals in one of these long, fast boats.

"Listen here," Sam growled. He spat over the side of the boat. "I've answered so many of your questions that I'm just going to give you one more answer. If you really want to know, I'll see to it that you find out, personally."

He looked James right in the eye. "Can you row?"

"Sure I can!" James said. In truth, he had become much stronger the past couple of weeks, thanks to all the hard work he had been doing on the ship.

"Then you'll find out soon enough!" said Sam.

He wouldn't say another word.

The *Bully Boy* was sailing south into whale country, and any day they expected to come across a school of whales. Sailors with the best eyesight were posted high up on the masts, with telescopes, to scan the horizons. Sure enough, early one sunny morning in July, a cry came down from the main mast, "Thar she blows!" They all rushed over to the side of the ship and saw, to the south, the white misty spouts of a school of sperm whales! James was so thrilled that he was rooted to the spot. His mouth fell open. It was Sam, rushing past him, who slapped him on the backside and got him out of his spell.

"Let's go!" he growled. "You said you could row!"

And before he knew it, James was in one of the long boats, along with several other sailors, an oar in his hand, being lowered down the side of the ship onto the water, and they were off! Eight rowed, powerfully, evenly, and they flew over the waves! Sam sat at the prow holding a deadly harpoon in one hand. The rope attached to it was carefully coiled in the bottom of the boat, then fastened again to the boat. The rowers had to be careful to keep their feet away from it.

James was excited. He had never worked so hard in his life, but he'd never felt so strong, either! They were getting closer to the gigantic beasts. More and more of them were surfacing like white mountains and their great white spouts seemed to rise a hundred feet in the air, all around the boat!

"Okay, men!" growled Sam. He braced his feet and drew back his harpoon. The first four rowers had stopped rowing and were removing the other harpoons from their places of safety under the seats. James strained around to watch Sam. Then a wave smashed into the side of the boat, sending all the rowers sliding sideways. James fell over on his side; his right foot became tangled in the coiled rope! As he struggled to sit up and free himself, he watched a harpoon fly from Sam's hand through the air towards the body of a huge, grey whale that rose from the sea like a shining, glistening mountain . . .

38

The seven stubbornest boys in the entire camp were in Bunk R. If they didn't want to do something, they usually didn't do it. "This bunk," their counselor, Terry, would yell at them, "is going to give me grey hair by the end of the summer! And you, especially, Tommy" (he would look at Tommy and make a face) "are particularly stubborn!"

The current problem concerned the weekly dance with the girls' camp, scheduled for the evening. Not one member of Bunk R wanted to go. Period.

"Why *not?*" Terry asked for about the tenth time.

"We don't like to dance," said Alan. He was the unofficial lawyer for the bunk. "And the music stinks!"

"All they play is that corny folk dance stuff like the Virginia Reel," said Tommy. "That's for hicks and people who wear shoes only on Sunday!"

"Very funny!" said Terry. "And I suppose you all know what'll happen if we don't show up for the dance *again?*"

No one felt like answering his question. The bunk had just gotten back from lunch and was reading comic books and playing cards when Terry entered, in a huff, as usual.

"*I'll* tell you what'll happen! Like the last dance. There'll be *too many extra girls hanging around!* You've *got* to go, boys!"

"But the girls are *ooky!*" Tommy yelled. Some of the guys laughed in agreement. "They're just *ooky!* I don't want to put my arms around any of *them!* Except for maybe you-know-who or what's-her-name."

"Yeah!" the other guys agreed. They knew who Tommy meant. There *were* a couple of nice and pretty girls. It didn't occur to them that the girls might have thought that most of the *boys* were from hunger, too. No, it just never occurred to them.

"Ooky, huh?" said Terry. "Ooky! Well, I'll figure out something. I'll be back in a few minutes."

He went out. Bunk R grumbled for a while, then went back to its card games and comics.

Ten minutes later Terry came back and for some reason he was carrying two small paper bags.

"All right!" he said in an official tone of voice. "Let's all assemble around here!" He sat down on one of the beds. The boys dropped their comics and cards and gathered around.

"This," said the counselor, "is what we are going to do tonight!" He shook the bags.

Silence. Bunk R members looked at each other. What the heck was he talking about?

"I have just talked to Bonnie," said Terry. (Bonnie was the counselor of the sister bunk.) "She and I agreed that since you guys don't want to cooperate, this is the way we are going to *do* it."

"Huh?" said Barry and Tommy at the same time.

"This is the fairest way for all concerned," said Terry. "Now, you see I have two paper bags here." He shook them again. "One has slips of paper with the names of the seven girls in Bonnie's bunk, and one has the names of *you* seven characters."

"Oh, no!" Tommy cried.

"Ah," said Terry, "you've caught on already! What I am going to do is pick a girl's name and a boy's name and you two will be a couple for the dance tonight. And if you don't cooperate . . . you know what'll happen!"

The way the boys carried on for two minutes, it seemed as if they had all gone out of their minds. They jumped on the beds, rolled on the floor, howled, threw pillows, stamped their feet.

Finally, they quieted down. Terry had them all over a barrel. The next day was Sunday—turkey-dinner-for-lunch-day. If they didn't cooperate, they'd get bologna sandwiches—again.

"Oh-kay!" said Terry. "Here's the first lucky fellow."

He reached one hand into each of the two bags and pulled out two slips of paper, "Pete," he called out, "and Anne."

"Gaak!" said Pete. "Her ears are so big she'll take off in a strong wind!"

"And next! Howard and . . . Helen!" Howard collapsed on the nearest bed, put a pillow over his head and moaned.

"Bill and Susan. Hazel and . . . Alan! Ha ha ha!" laughed Terry.

Alan glowered. Hazel was about four inches taller than Alan. Plus, she wasn't exactly Miss America; but Alan was not exactly Mr. Universe.

"Ruth and . . . what's this name? Oh, Bob!"

"Well," said Bob, "she ain't so bad." Ruth was quite pretty. None of the guys would publicly admit this to Terry, though.

"Now, who's left in these bags? Barry and Tommy" (he looked at Tommy, who made a face back) "and Rhonda and Jane."

"Oh, please," Tommy said to himself, "please don't let me get stuck with Jane! Not her! She ain't known as Calamity Jane for nothing. Oh, please . . . !"

Barry looked grim. He was probably thinking the same thing.

"The next girl's name is . . . Rhonda!" said Terry. "A very nice girl. And the lucky guy is . . . Barry!"

"Whew!" said Barry. "No Calamity Jane for *me!*"

Tommy went limp and fell backwards, groaning. Luckily there was a bed behind him.

"I *ain't* going!" he yelled.

39

Everybody told Tom and his wife that they were crazy to run off to California to dig for gold. But Tom and Ellen had read the stories in the papers about how the valuable metal had been discovered in big chunks near Sutter's Mill in 1848 and, as soon as they could, they sold their little grocery store, packed up all their goods in a wagon, and set out.

It was a long way to California from Chicago, Illinois. They had lots of company, too, for thousands of people were heading west to look for gold.

In May of 1849, Tom and Ellen reached San Francisco. They rested several days in the city and shopped for equipment and food. They bought shovels and picks and pans and camping supplies. Tom sold their horses and bought two sure-footed mules. They intended to go up into the hills, to prospect in the wilderness, where no one had dug before. The streams were cleaned out, they thought, and too many men and women were searching in the same places. They'd have better luck if they struck out on their own.

Tom bought a rifle to protect them from mountain lions, wolves, or bears and to hunt for fresh meat. He also bought two pistols, one for himself and one for Ellen. He had read and heard many stories about outlaws and bandits. California was not a state yet, it didn't have a strong government, so there weren't too many law enforcement officers around. "We've got to protect ourselves," Tom said to Ellen. "There are too many crooks around who'd steal what we spend weeks or months digging up."

He and his wife had no doubt that they would find a lot of gold and return, rich, to Chicago.

Tom and Ellen packed their supplies and equipment on the backs of their mules and headed up into the hills. They walked beside the mules and wore a pistol at the waist. The rifle was fastened to one of the packs where they could reach it quickly.

The afternoon of the ninth day, they came to a likely spot: a valley in which a shallow, briskly running stream had been eating away at the base of a crumbling, weathered, rocky hillside for many, many years.

"Let's try here," Ellen suggested. "If there was ever gold in the rocks of that hillside, it'll be in that stream right now!"

They set up camp on the shore. They let the mules roam about, for they wouldn't go very far and the vegetation they liked best to eat grew near the water.

Ellen and Tom had not seen another person for over a week. They were glad to be far away from San Francisco with its hustle and bustle and noise and hundreds of wagons and clouds of dust. For all they knew, no one except Indians had ever been in their beautiful valley, had ever stood on the bank of the stream and looked up to admire the blue sky, as blue as the finest turquoise.

"Let's take a sample," Ellen said eagerly. She put a shovel full of soil into the pan with some water and began to swirl the dirt around. Gradually the lighter dirt was washed out. She kept adding a little water until finally only the quartz gravel was left in the pan. She took the biggest pieces of quartz out with her fingers. In a few minutes all that remained in the pan was the finest, blackest, heaviest gravel. As she and Tom stared closely, she moved this pinch around in the light. Two or three tiny grains glowed like the sun.

Tom's heart thumped. "Look at that!" he said softly. "That's gold!"

Very, very early the next morning after breakfast, Ellen and Tom began to pan the soil of the stream. They knew that if they discovered what part of the stream had the heaviest gold flakes, they could then investigate the part of the hill right above the stream. Gold flakes were so heavy, they knew, that once they got washed down the hill, they didn't drift very far before settling.

Ellen and Tom were so absorbed in their quest they didn't notice that they forgot to stop to eat lunch, or that the sun, high in the sky, was reddening their skins. They panned shovelful after shovelful of stream gravel. By four o'clock they had decided there had to be only one place in the hill from which the gold had been washed down. They found quite a bit of gold dust, and a few little nuggets, in a stretch of stream only about fifteen feet wide. North of this area, and south of it, there was very little gold in the stream gravel.

"Well," said Tom, wiping his brow with the back of his hand, "now we know where to dig."

"Up there somewhere must be some gold!" Ellen said hopefully. She was tired, but she wasn't about to rest.

She and her husband looked up the hill. It was a rusty yellowish-brown in color and, here and there, a few dusty bushes managed to hang on.

"I'm going to use the pick up there," said Tom.

He took the sharp-pointed pick and scrambled, with some difficulty, up the steep hill. Dislodged pieces of quartz and dirt tumbled down after him.

"How about right here?" he asked. He was about ten feet below a clump of bushes. From this height, he could see a lot of the barren countryside. He secured his footing as well as he could, then raised the pick over his head and brought it down into the crumbling brown stone with a *smash!* He pulled it out and large pieces of crumbling quartz and dirt tumbled down the hill.

"Watch out!" he called.

Ellen scrambled out of the path of the falling rocks.

Smash! He drove the pick into the rock again. This time, the dislodged rock revealed something shiny and bright.

Tom fell to his knees and thrust his hands into the hole. "Ellen!" he managed to say.

Then he turned his head. Out of the corner of his eye he had caught a movement. Coming over the ridge, heading in the direction of the little valley, he saw three men on horses.

40

Blink! Blink! The red bulb flashed on and off, on and off. I couldn't move a muscle. My thoughts were unclear. Blink! Blink! On and off, on and off. I felt a tingling sensation in the toes of my left foot. It felt as if my foot had been frozen and was now thawing out. *Thawing out!* I thought. *Of course!* I tried to wiggle my toes, but I could not move those muscles. Not yet, I thought. Still too frozen.

My neck was stiff, too, so I was forced to look straight up at the ceiling. The tingling was beginning at the same time in many other parts of my body: my nose, then in my hands, then at the base of my spine and from there into my thighs. I tested the muscles of my hands and found I could just move the tips of my fingers.

My mind was thawing, too, and my thoughts were clearer now. I knew that it would be some time before I could move my body normally.

I *had* been frozen; but for how long I couldn't tell. I was certain of several things: that for years, or decades, or perhaps even centuries, I had been rocketing through space in an atomic starship at 90,000 miles a second, or almost half the speed of light, headed for a distant part of the universe, and that because I was being awakened, automatically, by the computer systems on the ship, I had reached the solar system of some distant star. I was now in orbit around a strange planet, one I would soon land on and explore.

I had been put to sleep, and frozen, my breathing and heartbeat slowed down nearly to zero, because the distance from Earth to the stars, even the nearest, is so great, that no man or woman could possibly live long enough to get there. Because I had been frozen, I had hardly aged at all. Only the instruments on the ship could tell me how long I had been asleep and how far I was from home. I thought to myself, the scientists who built my starship, the *Venturer*, the first ever designed to explore the distant universe, and the millions of people all over the earth who had watched the blast-off on television, were all long dead. Perhaps, I thought, no one on Earth remembered that I had been sent on this journey. I was on a one-way trip—I could never get back to Earth. And I was alone.

The computers on the *Venturer* had done a lot of experimenting and figuring before they decided to wake me up. First, of course, the *Venturer* had entered this solar system. Then, the computers had tested and measured each planet for the pull of its gravity, its radiation level, atmosphere and magnetic field. I was still frozen, asleep, when the *Venturer* went into orbit around the planet most like earth. And then even more careful, exact tests were performed. The atmosphere was tested for elements and water, radiation levels were carefully studied, even wind currents were recorded. After these tests, and dozens more, only then did the computers on the *Venturer* decide that it was safe to wake me up. If the planet had not been safe, the *Venturer* would have stored its information and, with me still asleep, would have gone on to another star, to another solar system, another planet.

After what seemed like several hours, I was able to move about and release myself from my special chamber. I stretched my stiff muscles, blinked, swallowed a few times and, after putting on a pair of boots with magnetic soles that gripped the floor of the ship, slowly made my way over to one of the instrument panels. I saw that I had been traveling, frozen and asleep, for two hundred and twenty-six years. Tears welled up in my eyes.

For several weeks I performed special exercises in the gym room of the *Venturer*. Every muscle of my body needed to be toned up. Some of the machinery in the gym was complicated and funny-looking, because it was designed to work on many muscles at the same time. When I first tried it out, on Earth, during my training period, I said to the scientists, "What kind of contraption is that? It looks like a combination of six bicycles turned upside-down, two tractors, and a lawn mower!" We all laughed. It wasn't such a funny joke now, though, as I had to spend several hours a day strapped into it. As I pressed different series of buttons on the control dial, the machine would stretch and release, stretch and release, different sets of muscles.

I was on a special diet. Of course, when I was frozen, I didn't eat anything. Tubes were attached to my veins, and I was fed small amounts of vitamins, minerals, and proteins to keep me alive. Now I was on a liquid diet. I even had some choices on my menu. For instance, I could choose between liquid turkey with stuffing and liquid ham and eggs.

In between exercise periods and sleep, I studied the planet. I had been trained to read the scientific instruments on the ship, so I was able to learn about the planet from the information gathered by the computers. I also had a telescope at my disposal. I saw that there was a lot of water on the surface of this planet, and that its oceans were blue, like Earth's. There were clouds in its atmosphere, but they weren't puffy. They floated in short, parallel dashes and dots, almost, I thought, like Morse code. The land was not green and brown, as Earth appeared from space, but violet-blue and black. The rivers were dark cracks on the surface. As I orbited around the planet, I saw several large lakes. What lived in them? I wondered. Who or what lived on that dark land?

Every three hours I strapped myself into a machine called the "Analyzer" so that the *Venturer*'s computers could test my body systems. Finally, after almost five weeks, the computers told me I was back in shape. Now it was time for me to board the small shuttle rocket which was tucked up against the hull of the *Venturer* like a folded wing. This would take me down to the surface of the new planet.

Many pieces of equipment were packed in the space shuttle: instruments to test air, food, and water, a microscope, tools to dissect animals and plants, bandages, a flashlight, a small inflatable rubber boat, even an umbrella! And, just in case the planet was inhabited by unfriendly beings, I carried a powerful stun gun.

I wore a space suit which I would discard soon after I landed. Carefully, I fitted myself into my narrow berth. I flipped a switch and a dial on the instrument panel, only inches from my face, began the countdown. The minutes and seconds ticked away. As "One Minute" flashed on in yellow letters, it suddenly occurred to me that I might die very soon. Then, I could no longer think; as "30 seconds" flashed on, the rocket engines and the vibrations shook the thoughts from my head.

20 seconds

10 seconds

9

8

7

6

5

4

3

2

1